THAT'S RACING!

also by
GEORGINA COLERIDGE

I Know What I Like

Georgina Coleridge

THAT'S RACING!
A Dream that Happened

HEINEMANN : LONDON

William Heinemann Ltd
15 Queen St, Mayfair, London WIX 8BE
LONDON MELBOURNE TORONTO
JOHANNESBURG AUCKLAND

First published 1978
© Georgina Coleridge 1978

434 14055 4

Printed & bound in Great Britain by
Cox & Wyman Ltd
London, Fakenham and Reading

*For Islay Mist and my partners
Frances, Arthur and Les, with love*

As costs keep increasing, all figures given here are approximate only.

G. C.

Extracts from *Racehorses* and *'Chasers & Hurdlers* annuals by kind permission of Timeform.

CONTENTS

1	My Kingdom for Half a Horse	1
2	We Galloped All Three	15
3	A Nod is as Good as a Blink	34
4	Shutting the Stable Door	49
5	The Trainer States the Following will not Run	68
6	A Horse of Another Colour	83
7	While the Grass Grows	100
8	If Wishes were Racehorses	109
9	Very Dark	119
10	You Can Take a Horse to the Water...	138

The author is very grateful indeed to Sarah Galbraith (super typing), Arthur Coleridge (general encouragement and punctuation), Alicia Yerburgh (brilliant editing), Auriol Sinclair (expert advice) and, of course, all those horses, thank you so much.

G. C.

I

My Kingdom for Half a Horse

Our family had no interest whatsoever in racing. Although my great-grandfather's blue and cream colours were registered in 1827 there is no record of any other link with racehorses. When my father lost a £100 bet at Ascot by a short head, he gave up in disgust. I was born and brought up mostly in East Lothian, twenty miles from Musselburgh where flat racing took place about once a year, and I had never seen a thoroughbred till we moved to a house near Guildford in 1932. Before that we lived for a time near Reigate and in March 1930 the grown-ups began to make plans to take seats on the special train to Aintree for the Grand National. As my birthday is in March, I quite wrongly assumed that they would include me, although I was only going to be fourteen, and my absolute fury at being left out may have caused the dream which showed me quite clearly that a horse called Shaun Goilin won. I decided not to tell anybody, but no sooner were they on the way to the station, than I began trying to discover how to bet with everyone in the house. The cook was appallingly indifferent, she had backed another horse anyway; the butler, a sepulchral character, did not 'hold with gambling'; but finally the gardener agreed to put on half-a-crown each way for me. He was a little startled when I explained that I only owned two shillings at the time, but sportingly accepted an IOU in case my dream came unstuck. History records that Shaun Goilin obliged at 100 to 8; what a beauty!

When all the family got home that night, full of Melleray's Belle (second) which they had all backed, it was strangely delightful to say: 'What bad luck, I was on Shaun Goilin.' Minor triumphs of this kind are wrapped in a very special quality and it must have been then and there that I first began to hanker after leading in a winner myself. It took me forty years.

Perhaps Merrylegs was really responsible, she taught me to love horses, to love riding, to love her, and the way that little Welsh Mountain pony influenced my sisters is rather extraordinary. Because of Merrylegs, my eldest sister Helen (Kemsley) breeds Welsh ponies in Leicestershire, my younger sister Daphne (Stewart) breeds Welsh ponies in Berwickshire and the youngest, Frances (Pearson), my racing partner, breeds Welsh ponies in South Wales. It all started on my fifth birthday.

We lived in a large house near the Lammermuirs in East Lothian, where the children could be fitted tidily into a pagoda-shaped wing, linked to the main building by a long, narrow, inky-dark passage with a swing door at one end. We called the journey from the nursery to the domain of the grown-ups 'going through' and always ran, holding our breath, to the swing door, dashing into the warm, cigarette-tinged atmosphere of the front hall as the door swung shut behind us with a hollow thump. In those days parents were a remote and separate entity, apt to expect verses to be recited, questions to be answered and perfect behaviour – including clean fingernails, so a tinge of apprehension went along with us every time we 'went through'.

On my birthday I dashed headlong down the dreaded

passage, hurtled into the hall, on into the dining-room where my present was sure to be. My father was eating his breakfast, but there was no sign of a parcel on the table. I was kissed on the head jerkily as usual and wished a Happy Birthday, then Pop said: 'Go along to the front door now and tell me what's there.' This seemed quite unreasonable and I knew it was impossible to turn the heavy brass handle on the door leading into the conservatory which would have to be negotiated first.

'I can't open it,' I said.

'Go on and try,' said Pop briskly.

So, with a sulky face, hating every minute, I ran down to the hall to struggle with the door-handle. Pop had followed, so he helped.

'Go on, open the front door now.'

I struggled again, the lock wouldn't budge but at last, with a little assistance, I jerked it open and there standing outside was a huge brown paper parcel with my name on it. Jimmy Laurie who drove the dogcart was there too. The parcel moved.

'Open your parcel,' said Pop. 'Come on.'

Inside the brown paper was Merrylegs, my very own live pony. The excitement, delight and utter surprise are unforgettable. Love at first sight – for a beautiful bright bay Welsh Mountain pony with a white star on her forehead, a tiny white mark on her velvet nose, a long black mane and tail, black legs, already wearing a saddle and bridle. A photograph taken on that wonderful morning shows me in a white cotton dress, a jersey, and a seraphic smile riding Merry (I couldn't manage the whole name) for the first time.

Our friendship lasted twenty-three years. Merrylegs taught me to ride and to get on again when she bucked me off; she always waited, looking at me quizzically till I climbed up again, but like so many good horses she had maddening quirks. It took half an hour and four people to catch her and she once jumped a gate as tall as herself to escape – but she was absolutely sure-footed and, although high spirited, a perfect child's pony.

A nasty surprise was my first and only term at a boarding school near London, where I found myself being pushed into thick woollen vests and extraordinary navy blue knickers with separate white linings. I was so devastated at parting with Merrylegs that she was allowed to come to school too, which created quite a sensation. No one else had brought a pony, I was the proud owner and could give people rides – poor Merrylegs became harder and harder to catch and it sometimes took the whole class to corner her.

It was a school where anyone with a title seemed to do well, and my mother noted that I (aged nine) was top in French, spelling and composition, while Helen (aged eleven and a half) was top in history, English and general knowledge. This unlikely achievement as far as I was concerned, seemed to spell Teacher's Pet in large letters – so I was taken away in the nick of time back to a world of governesses, Nanny and of course Merrylegs. At times we came to London, where riding in the Row made it essential for me to own tidy jodhpurs. I never owned anything so suitable again. I suppose it was enjoyable, but it bore no resemblance to real riding, which for me meant meandering through the eternal beauty of the beechwoods, with the flutter of birds, the scent of damp leaves, the wild garlic and the primroses. From behind the nursery wing at Yester a narrow, rough, muddy track ran for about two miles along the burn to the Lammermuirs and this was by far my favourite ride.

It was on Merrylegs that I spent my most enchanted summer's day. The track followed the burn over seven little stone bridges to Danskine Loch and the hills beyond. Merrylegs and I often went 'up Danskine'. After a sunny, bright green expanse of rough grass, grazed flat by hundreds of rabbits, the path crossed the first bridge into the deep, dark shade of beech trees, so tall, so thickly planted that the sky hardly showed through and their cool, damp welcome came as a delicious surprise. We always cantered across the open space, then walked, day-dreaming, under the great trees with the burn tracing its gentle rustling journey from the hills, crossing and recrossing our path. We rode near the ruins of Yester Castle, locally known as the Goblin Hall, which, from a hillock surrounded by a loop in the burn, originally defended the glen. A steep path over yet another bridge led up to the castle, but we never went there, because it was altogether too spooky. Usually Merry broke into a brisk trot well before the castle bridge, passing into more friendly territory as quickly as possible, but that day it was so hot that she simply lengthened her elegant stride, her little hooves silent on the grassy track. Suddenly she stopped, ears pricked: we were surrounded by a herd of roedeer. For about thirty seconds they stayed in a rare shaft of sunlight, grazing by the burn with their calves, then, as if blown like butterflies on the breeze, they melted away, rippling over fallen trees and bushes in graceful, magic leaps and we were alone again. Merrylegs and I had been among the roedeer. I still relive those dreamlike moments with the same deep delight — they were so beautiful, so wild and so utterly free — we never saw them again.

My tidy jodhpurs were in evidence when Merrylegs won second prize at Haddington Show. For a week I polished her, combed her long mane, combed her long tail, shined her hooves and gave her so much corn that she got completely out of hand. If Helen hadn't kept a tight hold of her as we went into the ring, goodness knows where I would have landed. I was very proud of my blue prize card, which was quickly nailed up in the harness-room, among the cobwebs and dust, beside the stuffed head of a famous trotting mare. My great-grandfather was horse mad. He drove all over the country with an unbeatable tandem pair of big, black hackneys.

Our great-grandfather may have been brilliant, and he was certainly successful, living to be nearly a hundred – after becoming a Field Marshal and being Governor of Madras. Raeburn's portrait shows him as a magnificently good-looking young man with black curly hair, blue eyes and powerful shoulders. He was thoroughly unpleasant, however – sadistic and brutal to his fourteen children. On the credit side, a dedicated forester, he planted thousands of beech trees along the glen to create the spectacular beech bank which I loved so much.

The only remotely human story I know about him came from Dr Martine, our family doctor. He said that one morning a famous wrestler was driving south through the Lammermuirs after winning a championship contest in Edinburgh, when he saw a tandem trotting up the glen towards him. His own trotters were unbeaten in many races, so he hurried to reach the narrow bridge half a mile ahead where the river marked the county boundary. There was room for only one cart there. My great-grandfather saw the other tandem flying along, so he raced for the bridge too and the horses met, blowing hard, head on. Neither would go back. In the end the men got down without a word, unhitched the horses and fought it out. Two hours later the wrestling champion was revived by a passing shepherd. As he came round he said: 'There's only two persons could have knocked me out, one is the devil himself, and the other's yon other devil, the Marquis of Tweeddale.'

I loved our stables, with all the old harness covered in cobwebs. One year I spent some of my Christmas money on pale blue and cream paint to decorate Merrylegs's loose-box in the family colours.

By the end of the summer I was growing fast, so Pop suggested that Merrylegs should be sent to the stud, now that she was too small for me and too lively for my younger sister to ride. Daphne, who was seven, owned a donkey which she had bought for sixpence from a gypsy on the village green. A sight to remember was my sister, who was very small for her age, leading a huge brown donkey stallion up the front drive under Nanny's disapproving frown, which was completely outdone by the French governess's cries of: *'Mais il est charmant!'* Charming was just what that horrible donkey was not. He bit like a rat-trap, dashing at anyone who came within reach, his ears laid back, huge yellow fangs bared, but he loved my sister because, we guessed, he must have believed her to be his fairy godmother who had rescued him from the gypsies. She called him Bunny. All was well until he bit the postman severely as the man bicycled past without even looking towards him. Pop ruled that another less dangerous donkey must be found and Bunny was returned to the gypsies.

Meanwhile, we were lent a grey mare called Misty, a good size bigger than Merrylegs, which was alleged to be quiet to ride and drive. A day or two later we set off in the dogcart to fetch the new donkey from a farm about ten miles away, with a picnic included in the general excitement. Anyone who has tried to lead a small, ultra slow, reluctant, elderly and tedious donkey for ten miles, will understand why it was dark before we got home, each of us (not Nanny – she never touched anything bigger than Pupsy, my peke, who sat on her lap throughout) exhausted and bad tempered. However, the donkey, Susan, seemed to be the ideal harness partner for the new pony. Without giving the idea much consideration, we harnessed them into a miniature Victoria the next day and set off with the tortoise-like donkey acting as a brake for the erratic behaviour of the 'quiet to ride and drive' Misty, who kept attempting a sharp, excitable canter while Susan plodded along – the epitome of disagreeable reluctance.

That day four of us were supposed to be picking wild raspberries to make lovely jam, which, being translated into our terms, meant eating a lot of wild raspberries. There were never quite enough to pick, particularly after we had tasted them all, just to make sure they were ripe. Helen and the cousins decided to leave me to look after the transport and I soon got bored trying to keep the pony quiet by feeding it handfuls of grass. Finally, in a fidget, I unhitched the donkey, tied it to the fence and drove off with the pony harnessed alone to one side of the pole. It had not occurred to me that a very steep hill that led to an S-bend on a bridge near the house would be dangerous. The slope was 1 in 4, so I slammed on the metal brake which made a ghastly grinding noise, thoroughly startling the pony. It tore off at a mad gallop down the hill. We hit both sides of the stone bridge, bounced onto the flat road beyond and careered towards an exceptionally solid wooden gate set into stone pillars. Part of the gate shattered as the pole met it and the pony's weight crashed through the rest, but the impact flung the Victoria over onto its side with me underneath. The noise brought the farm workers to the rescue, and the pony was unscrambled with hardly a scratch. 'Where's the other pony?' they asked incredulously. 'You were never driving the one pony in a two-horse cart?' No one asked if I was all right. My shoulder was absolutely numb and there was mud all over me from the wet patch at the gate, which had probably saved the pony and me from being badly smashed (this accident helped me to understand how jockeys survive being galloped over after a fall). I ran home and got into the bath, where Nanny found me admiring the most enormous bruises anyone had ever seen on a small arm, but this seemed quite unimportant compared with the filthy state of my clothes.

Soon after that I decided to ride the grey pony. We always left the saddle on the gate, caught our pony, climbed on board and rode up the field. I clambered onto the creature, kicked it gently in its fat ribs and was sent flying straight onto a stone. My collar-bone cracked and a loud voice called out: 'Come here to me.' It was John Brown, the head gamekeeper, who kept an eye on us when our parents were away. 'Let me see that arm,' he said. 'Move it.' I couldn't. In a matter of seconds I was sitting in his car (a model T Ford with sensational charm) on the way to Haddington to see Dr Martine. He told me I had broken my collar-bone and that it must be X-rayed in Edinburgh. I was furious – what a fuss about a simple fall in a field, but I found myself being driven to Edinburgh without any lunch because of the beastly grey pony. 'Why do you make me do all this, when I haven't had my lunch and this shoulder doesn't hurt half so much as the other one,' I said, trying not to cry with rage. At once Dr Martine said: 'What's this about your other shoulder?' And of course it had been broken too. This caused great satisfaction because one broken collar-bone gave me the privilege of wearing a brown leather sling, quite a rarity in a non-riding district, while the second collar-bone was a superb grievance to hold over Nanny. It was lovely to boast about. I made the most of it. Mummy, who was back in London by then, hearing that my left clavicle had been fractured, assumed that I was suffering from a broken leg, so she panicked and sent for me to come south. This gave me a thrilling journey in a sleeper – first class – all by myself, except for Pupsy, the peke, who never left my side (unless ponies were around – he had strong views about them). Mummy was very put out when she discovered that I had such a minor injury, but told the story against herself for years.

When I was twelve, Merrylegs produced Foalie, who put the seal on my devotion to horses and taught me to be patient – the only quality essential for racehorse owners. One April day he was there beside her, a comic, black, woolly toy horse on springs, bucking around his mother and generally showing off whenever I came near. Unfortunately dear Merrylegs did not propose to be caught and it became obvious that a special plan would be needed if I was ever going to touch the foal. After a few days it struck me that he was very inquisitive and only his mother's evasive tactics prevented him from letting me get within reach. Hoping hard, I filled a paper bag with the nursery sugar and went to sit on the grass in the field waiting, my fingers smeared with sugar and held out absolutely still for an hour. After three days Foalie came closer and closer, but it took almost a week before his soft, velvety black muzzle prodded my fingers delicately and found that they tasted sweet. Foalie started to lick them. It took another three weeks before we were firm friends, after that Merrylegs had to follow us. Foalie thought I was simply splendid.

One whistle from the gate was enough to bring him careering across the field like a mad black puffball, bucking and neighing – to stand on his hindlegs, front feet on my shoulders, asking for sugar. Foalie learnt to shake hands, to curl up his nose, to kneel down, to roll over and eventually to walk, trot or canter to order and even to take people's hats off. In the end he once walked right up the front stairs at Yester and quietly down again for a bet. Several times he came into the dining-room to turn his nose up for sugar when there were guests to admire him. Foalie liked plenty of attention and came for long walks, with Merrylegs fussing along behind, quite annoyed at the way her child had developed such advanced ideas.

One bright cold May day, huge snowflakes swirled down in a freak storm and Foalie was enchanted with them. He trotted round, mouth open, trying to catch them as they fell. He then gave up to lick them off his mother's thick coat. I longed for a camera to capture his intense look of interest in the snowflakes and his puzzled expression when they melted under his very nose. The same afternoon there was nearly a disaster. A relative staying in the house owned a young chow which snapped and snarled at our dogs and at everyone except her. I was sure the brute would chase Foalie and decided to patrol the stable field. I was leaning on the gate, just about to whistle up Foalie when the chow ran into a corner of the field from the woods. My heart began to thump uncontrollably as the dog launched itself towards the ponies. Merrylegs swung round snorting, ready to go into action, but I had underestimated the little foal. He was, after all, a stallion, aware of his territorial rights, and he went straight for that dog, bucking, squealing and kicking! The chow turned tail and fled.

When we moved to Surrey in 1930, Foalie came too and I spent hours driving him in long reins along the roads to get him used to the traffic, and breaking him in. When he was eighteen months old, I took him to the blacksmith to have his first tiny shoes fitted. He was not much bigger than a Great Dane and looked absolutely angelic. The smithy was run by gigantic twin brothers – and they laughed at me when I led in my little pony and offered to stay while he was pedicured. 'He can be rather playful,' I said.

'Run along my girl and leave him to us, he's just a toy – collect him in an hour.'

An hour later the pony, dripping in sweat, was standing there unshod, while the two giants, perspiring at every pore, sat mopping their foreheads. Every time a huge hand touched his leg the pony stood straight up on end. No matter what they tried – he stood up time and time again. I had unfortunately taught him to walk on his hind legs if I touched his knee. However, one only had to say 'stand still' in a quiet voice and he always did. They had shouted 'whoa there' and a lot else that he had not heard before. With a withering glance at the men, I said 'stand still' and picked up a perfectly willing little foreleg. 'Goodness, he hasn't got his shoes yet,' I said. 'Have you been very busy?' They made the shoes in record time with hardly a word and when we left, the more vocal brother said:

'I have never seen anything like that little fellow, next time don't leave him here.'

In 1932 we moved to Guildford – Foalie and all, because Helen was now seventeen which meant the approach run up to her debut in London society, a subject about which we knew nothing whatsoever. We had always lived in Scotland, or abroad, so the social world had never been discussed. By a sheer stroke of luck, one of my father's friends, hearing that I had nothing to ride, asked if I would like an ancient Argentine pony called Jane, who had played international polo and was a perfect ride. She arrived the following week and, although totally unsound and pretty frail, was a marvellous new asset – my first grown-up horse.

The only other occupant of the stables was the Platypus who had been bought straight out of a baker's van for my Aunt K to potter about on. He was perhaps the result of an unfortunate meeting between a Welsh cob and a Shire mare because he had a huge roman-nosed head, colossal flat feet, and a very weird short-backed physique. The Platypus had only two paces – a dead-slow walk or a ponderous, bone-shaking trot. He could be persuaded into his own special version of a canter, but no one repeated this experiment on purpose. My first attempt at hunting was on the broad back of the Platypus, because Jane was too old for violent exercise. That once was more than enough.

We arrived at the meet safely – after pausing outside every village shop – habit dies hard with horses and the Platypus was most conscientious. He perked up visibly on seeing a lot of horses, hounds and people, but that was nothing to the antics that followed. In his own elephantine way he went at full speed, lolloping madly through muddy paths among the rhododendrons, absolutely out of control, slipping and sliding in and out of wet ditches (he never tried to jump them, but plodded cheerfully right in up to his tummy) and I was just getting used to this unacceptable form of sport when we were faced with a very small wooden fence which everyone else hopped over effortlessly. Not us – oh no. The Platypus stopped dead, nearly bringing down three innocent people who were queueing up in the narrow space behind us, and only just failing to shoot me over his thick head. Then, snorting and puffing, he stepped over first with one huge foot, then the other, and stopped again. After a most embarrassing pause – which seemed like hours – there was a shattering of timber as he dragged his hind legs through, one at a time, after him. Never again.

One morning I ambled off on Jane to explore a bridle path leading to Newlands Corner where we had heard that there was lovely riding country, and suddenly came upon a string of elegant, beautiful, skinny-looking horses, with little cloth-capped men perched on their backs. As I came up to the last man I asked: 'Are those racehorses?' 'The owners seem to think so,' he said, 'better ask the Guv'nor.' It didn't take me long to discover that we had come to live near Peter Thrale, a very successful trainer of steeplechasers and hurdlers. Next morning, with the persistence of youth, I rode up to his front door, rang the bell and, not realizing the extent of my impertinence, calmly asked to be shown round the stables! Mrs Thrale was pardonably surprised and not too pleased at a scruffy-looking teenager turning up out of the blue with such a request, but Peter, who was having breakfast, overheard and called me in.

'I can't leave the pony, sorry,' I shouted back, 'there's nowhere to tie her to.'

'Wait a bit then,' he said and soon appeared, wiping his mouth on a huge red handkerchief. Peter Thrale had the most tremendous twinkle in his eye and his whole expression seemed to be looking for laughter. He was very like a prosperous farmer, and just the sort of person I had pictured as a trainer — thick-set, quiet-voiced, unhurried, he was one of the kindest people I ever met. Within a few minutes I was invited to ride out next day with Peter and our friendship lasted till he died in 1959.

2

We Galloped All Three

Riding out with Peter Thrale's string was invariably great fun. My eldest sister Helen, who was very good on a horse, often rode work on some of the hurdlers, and an old 'chaser called Forearmed. He was a plain, gaunt creature with a strong sense of the ridiculous, who threw whoever rode him at least once – if not every single time. Forearmed was the stable favourite. He had won eleven races, including turning out to win two days running at Sandown which is really unusual. Peter asked us if we would like to have him 'for a good home' and we were thrilled because Helen had nothing to ride, but I swapped my share against her stamp collection as Jane was still going strong, and riding Forearmed did not appeal to me – he was far too awkward.

Forearmed had a fine eye to his audience, and just when one least expected it, he would give a hitch of his powerful quarters, drop his shoulder and throw his rider head first onto the floor. He would then stand looking down as if shocked and surprised at such antics.

I found this rather funny, but vowed that on no account would I allow the old devil to drop his shoulder like that if I ever had to ride him – a prospect that was less than attractive. Eventually there was no escape when Helen went away for the week-end, so I had to climb onto Forearmed's bony heights, gather up the reins firmly and start towards the gallops. His lazy, slack thoroughbred stride was peculiar after Jane's amble, and his long, thin neck seemed apt to disappear if one did not constantly make him keep his head up. We joined the string safely enough, then, with typical bravado, I asked if I could canter with some of the hurdlers (who were doing slow work that morning). Peter grinned, looking at me on my unfamiliar mount.

'You can,' he said, tapping his teeth with his whip. 'You can, but remember Forearmed enjoys his little joke. Don't let him get away with you now.'

Feeling closely related to the boy who stood on the burning deck, I followed two hurdlers down to the start without any trouble, deciding that it would be wise to settle my horse behind them. This master plan lasted for about one minute, after which Forearmed, pulling my arms out, pushed between the other two, bumping first the one on the left, then the one on the right.

'Keep him straight, Miss.'

'Look out, Miss, keep him straight,' shouted the lads politely. Forearmed bumped and bored his way up the gallop at a far from slow canter and as soon as we were within earshot I heard Peter yelling:

'Steady, pull up, steady on there.' As we reached Peter's vantage point, Forearmed swerved wildly towards him, stopped dead and decanted me on my feet, breathless, scarlet-faced, but intact, beside his hack. Peter laughed so much that he nearly fell off too. I was never allowed to forget it.

When my sister Frances, aged five, had learnt to ride on Foalie, aged four, she kept asking to come out with the racehorses. Peter said she could if I kept Foalie on the leading rein, and Frances was in her seventh heaven. The excitement was almost unbearable, but Foalie seemed to take the expedition very calmly, trotting along beside Jane, until the point at which seven very green two-year-olds appeared on the scene to walk round in a circle before starting work. Foalie's little ears pricked, he snorted, pawed the ground and standing up on end, let out a resounding squealing neigh, challenging all comers to instant battle. The two-year-olds scattered in all directions, three lads fell off, Peter's language reached unscaled flights, and I hurled myself from Jane to restrain the guilty party. Foalie was led home in disgrace. Some months later Peter said: 'You can bring the pony out tomorrow with the old horses, but hang onto the little blighter.' Foalie, looking as sweet as pie, Frances smiling blissfully, parked themselves beside Peter on his hack (Polly) to watch the gallops. We were concentrating on a group of horses coming towards us very fast when there was a squeaky yelp from Frances as Foalie rolled on the ground. – he was feeling rather too hot and had got tired of waiting. Polly shied violently at the sight of Foalie's four legs waving in the air. Jane, outraged, pulled away from me as I leapt off to rescue Frances from the general muddle. Total disorder reigned as the racehorses swerved all over the place – that was final. No more riding out for Foalie.

One day Peter said he would take me to a National Hunt (jumping) meeting at Sandown. This was a tremendous excitement and rather bewildering, because I had never seen a racecourse, except at the cinema where the newsreels showed the Grand National and the Derby. Peter disappeared towards the Weighing Room, after giving me two shillings and whispering 'Essex Beacon'. There I stood in a strange world, wondering how to place my bet. At last I discovered Tattersalls, and plucking up my courage, chose an elderly bookie with a walrus moustache.

Luckily he accepted my two shillings on Essex Beacon with a broad grin, without pointing out that I was obviously under age, and handed me a betting slip. I clutched that bit of cardboard as if it had been solid gold and mooched around, worrying in case I would never find Peter again, when at last the horses appeared on their way to the start. Peter's horse won at 12 to 1, what a beauty, transforming my finances from nil to twenty-four shillings. I think it was on that day, at Sandown, that my ambition to own a racehorse came alive again.

Sometimes a proud owner arrived to exercise his own horse, which could be a severe trial for Peter. One particularly aggressive gentleman with a fine moustache addressed him like a public meeting while inspecting the stables. He was very confident indeed about his chances of winning an amateur race and had come to ride his horse at exercise as a dress rehearsal. Peter had not seen him on horseback before and I noted a quizzical expression spreading over his face as the Major boomed on, finally disappearing with the string, sitting bolt upright, supremely confident, towards the gallops. While we waited for the riders to loom out of the mist, I asked if the horse had a real chance. 'With anyone else riding of course it could win,' said Peter. 'But that fella would stop a church.' The Major came up the gallops at a steady pace, bolt upright in the saddle, with the horse absolutely out of control and together they disappeared at the same steady pace into the blue. I heard next day that the horse had found its way home a good deal later, with the Major full of explanations about the scotch mist making the reins slippery.

Another owner, very smart, very professional looking, rode out regularly, flicking his immaculate boots with his immaculate riding-whip and appearing to need absolutely no advice on any subject. But he had not yet ridden in a race. Peter politely suggested that, as his horse took a very strong hold on the racecourse, a pair of gloves would be helpful. 'I don't wear gloves,' said the owner.

'They help,' said Peter.

'I don't wear gloves.'

No more was heard on the subject. I duly went to the races again (with much more confidence) with Peter, who had four runners. On the way he said: 'Wish the bloody fool would listen.' Evidently the episode of the gloves still rankled. Winning the first race at 6 to 1 put Peter in a better frame of mind (I was highly delighted – my two shillings each way had become a respectable sum). He won the next race too at 6 to 4 – not quite so spectacular financially, but comfortable. The fourth race came at last and the owner, immaculate as ever (without gloves) rode the favourite onto the course to canter to the start. Peter's two previous winners had helped to bring the price down to 2 to 1 on, but I knew he was extremely worried and with good reason. There was a gasp from the crowd as the horse sailed past the starting gate at a relentless gallop and went on to do a complete circuit of the course. There was a long pause, during which Peter swore under his breath without stopping, as horse and rider came past the winning post the wrong way and rejoined the waiting field, only to go past them again. But this time rather more slowly. With a desperate last effort, the unhappy rider managed to stop and turn the horse round just as the tapes went up, and they were off again. To everyone's relief the horse won.

I added to my loot when one of the hurdlers Helen sometimes rode came second, paying 59/6 for 2/- on the Tote. Pop, seeing me emptying my handbag onto the drawing-room floor that evening to count the swag (I had amassed about £11) said that if Mr Thrale was likely to win again at any time, he would be obliged if I would put £1 on for him. This was a great step forward, because up till then my craze for racing had been frowned upon, although once or twice week-end guests had been taken to see the horses. Some time later Peter had a very good chance to win a steeplechase, so I told Pop. He solemnly handed me a whole pound note to bet with on his behalf, which I carried to the £1 window of the Tote, feeling as if all eyes were upon me. The horse was a hot favourite again but, horror of horrors, it fell at the third fence. This would have been easier to bear if Peter's disregarded runner in the last race had not won at 8 to 1. I thought it advisable not to mention that my two shillings had been on that.

The second time I went hunting it was my winnings, which I regarded as 'Horse Money', that took me. In those days you could hire a horse for 12/6. So having saved up the necessary, I went by bus to Guildford to find myself a hunter for next Saturday's meet. My plan was a deadly secret. I owned only ghastly jodhpurs, a grubby macintosh and an elderly bowler hat (discarded by Helen in favour of a smart new replacement). At the stable I found a small, pale-faced, red-haired man in breeches and leather gaiters and said: 'I would like to hire a horse for Saturday at Chiddingfold.' He gazed at me sadly.
 'What sort of horse do you ride?'
 'Well I've got an old polo pony, but she's no good for hunting, I want a quiet horse that jumps everything.'
 'Our horses are quiet all right, and they all jump.'
 'Can I have a look round?' It was very dark in the stables and not very tidy, but the horses were plump and more like Peter's hack than anything else. I chose the biggest, because it was the best looking.
 'You don't want a huge horse like that, my dear,' said the man, who had been watching as I looked searchingly at each horse in turn. 'He'd carry two of you and never notice. He's all of seventeen hands, but he's very quiet.'

'I'll have that one,' I said firmly – 'Please, on Saturday at Chiddingfold crossroads.'

'That'll be fifteen shillings,' he said, equally firmly. I counted out the money with such reluctance that he said: 'I'll bring him there all right, my dear. I've three more going.'

My heart sank on the way to the meet, but Helen's astonishment at the size of my horse with me perched on top comforted me a little. It felt just like driving a three-ton lorry after riding a bicycle. Whereas Jane spun on a sixpence, and responded instantly to the lightest touch, my elephantine choice lumbered along, head down, leaning heavily on the bit and the earth seemed to shake under us as he cantered with ponderous determination in the wake of whichever horse he elected to follow. I had absolutely no choice, but at such a slow pace felt perfectly safe and began to enjoy myself. The hunt spent a long time hanging about on a sandy heath, where occasionally one or two enterprising types would gallop off, to return quite soon. We idled there in the sun for about two hours. Then the hunt moved on along a narrow road between grass fields, everyone trotting purposefully behind. Suddenly hounds were away along the edge of a field and we broke into a mad gallop. I ended up facing a wooden five-barred gate which seemed quite small from the heights of my huge horse. So, without the slightest hesitation, I tapped him down the shoulder and kicked him with both heels. He took a terrific leap at the gate, sending me flying straight over his head into (luckily) a deep sea of wet mud. One large hoof trod on my shoulders, another large hoof cut a neat semi-circle out of my bowler. Once again I was saved by the mud. It must have been a fine sight, but I was comparatively unscathed, although the bruises were spectacular when examined in the bathroom mirror and my back ached for weeks. I wisely jettisoned the bowler, pretending to have lost it.

It was a very muddy home-coming, but that first real fall laid the foundation for my sympathetic admiration for all those National Hunt jockeys who risk their lives dozens of times every day, in fact at every fence. There was no more hunting for me that year. My mother was furious about my adventure and said it must not be repeated. My father thought it a great joke, however, but suggested that it was hardly fair to expect to jump a gate from a standstill on a strange horse. 'Or didn't it occur to you that the horse could have had a beastly fall?'

That had never entered my head. Merrylegs had always hopped over any obstacle she met — fallen trees, ditches, low hedges were all one to her. I had not been taught to jump, or even how jumps should be approached. So the number of falls grew with the number of times I went hunting.

We had been riding out regularly for some time, when one morning Mrs Thrale called me over to the house as I trotted up to the stables. Peter was ill — too ill to accompany an important owner, who was due to arrive at any moment to see his horse do a full-speed gallop.

'You look after him, Georgina, Peter says you know all the horses. See that he gets there, and show him where to stand. Peter wants him to ride Polly.' I took my responsibility very seriously, never having spoken to an owner before. Polly was Peter's hack, a hideous, ex-milk-cart pony with only one recognizable pace, a bouncy, clattering, very slow, but somehow menacing canter. She had a huge head, a thickly arched neck and powerful quarters and liked to proceed with her head in the air, snorting and puffing. Peter weighed about fifteen stone, so she suited him admirably; she also stood still to watch the gallops and was just like a bicycle to him.

The owner was a slight little man with grey hair, most unsuitably dressed in a navy blue suit, stiff white collar and city tie, black shoes and socks and a black felt hat! He got out of a colossal Rolls-Royce with the help of a very grand chauffeur and was dismayed to learn that the only way to the gallops was either on foot or on Polly's ugly back.

One of the lads helped Mr Brown to climb up and we set off. Polly was quite unaccustomed to a lightweight jockey, so she started a series of trial bounces at which Peter would have shouted: 'Shut up you fool and behave yourself.' Mr Brown went pale, clutched the reins and said:

'I have not been on a horse for years, my dear, is this one always such a rough ride?'

Leaning forward, I grabbed Polly's nose-band. 'Shut up you silly old fool,' I shouted in her ear. 'Shall I lead her till she settles down?' I asked politely.

'Thank you very much, my dear,' said Mr Brown. So I carefully led the infuriated Polly up the path, Jane for once laying her ears back, as Polly plunged along, frustrated and fuming.

It seemed like hours before we got to the end of that narrow path and I was sweating as much as Jane – but we made it and joined the string where Polly carried Mr Brown to Peter's usual vantage point, standing like a Police Horse, as if butter wouldn't melt in her mouth. I foresaw trouble on the way back. Peter always cantered sharply home to be there as the string returned, so that every horse could be looked over with his eagle eye before it was unsaddled – oh dear, what would Polly do when the time came? I had a brilliant wheeze: 'Mr Brown,' I asked tentatively, 'would you like me to ride Polly back while you ride Jane? I think you would like her better, she ambles along very comfortably.' He was delighted and we swopped horses. Jane could hardly believe her eyes – Polly was equally outraged. Suddenly the galloping horses came into view, at first very small nearly a mile away, gradually coming nearer till we could hear the lads' voices, then they were racing past to pull up at the top of the slope on our right. Polly took me over to the horses after the gallop, Jane following meekly with Mr Brown – far less harassed-looking by now, able to take a real interest in his horse which the head lad led up, puffing as it walked round us, steaming all over, and generally giving the impression that the gallop had been thoroughly testing.

At this point, Polly started edging away towards home, so I took a very firm grip indeed on the reins, at the same time taking Jane by the bridle to bring the two horses together for the stormy passage back to base. After a few attempts at getting away with me, Polly gave an angry snort and settled into a most uncomfortable, slogging trot. I now saw just why Peter allowed her to canter at all times, but did not dare give an inch in case I was removed bodily from Mr Brown. We got back safely and in triumph after a hectic slither down the shortest route I knew; saying a thankful goodbye to my protégé, now on firm ground again and pink with his exertions.

Three weeks later a typewritten envelope came addressed to me. I had never seen my name typewritten before and nobody except Granny ever wrote to me. I turned it upside down, held it to the light and irritated the nursery party considerably by going off to the stables to open it in Jane's loose-box. The letter was from Mr Brown's secretary. It enclosed two badges and a car park label and invited me to join him for lunch in his box for the Derby. There could be few greater moments in a racing-mad sixteen-year-old's life than that. I rushed to show it to Pop. 'Ask your mother,' he said, as he always did. 'I don't know Mr Brown. Where on earth did you meet him?' I told him of Jane's rescue operation and he thought the story hilarious, so much so that he came to find Mummy to share the joke with her. Typically, she said I was far too young to go anywhere at all in public and on no account could I go to a race meeting with a young man.

'But he's very old,' I said, 'with white hair and very rich. He has a huge Rolls and a chauffeur with gold buttons.' Pop was asked to discover all about Mr Brown, but my life was saved by Aunt K who came into the room at the crucial moment, heard the words: 'Derby in a box with a strange man — impossible,' and on being told the whole saga said:

'Why shouldn't she accept, but say you don't let her go out alone as she is only sixteen, can she bring me as her chaperone — I'd love it.' Saved again. We had a wonderful time, and I even backed the winner with two shillings each way, kindly donated by Peter Thrale, who was tickled all colours of pink by the thought that his important owner had been so pleased. This introduction to flat racing could hardly have been more perfect, and my racing head was turned by the grandeur of the Derby. Ever afterwards the family teased me about it: 'Georgina only goes racing in a box — Georgina only goes racing with millionaires.' It was fun to be in such an enviable situation.

My life was interrupted for a while by the inescapable ritual of becoming a thoroughly reluctant, not to say Bolshie debutante. Anyone less fitted to wear long white gloves and make polite conversation to strange young men (unless by some God-sent chance they liked racing) could hardly be imagined. This was also the era of weekend parties in big country houses. Luckily for me, the first one I went to on my own was in Scotland, where I had the good fortune to meet a young couple who lived at Newmarket, where he ran a small, but successful racing stable. I joined in a poker game without asking what stakes were being played for, and immediately lost £5 worth of chips, thinking they were worth five shillings (my father did not allow anyone to gamble for more). My host's face when I asked for another five bob's worth was a study in absolute embarrassment. I stopped playing, aghast. My total assets at the time being a return ticket to Haddington and one pound, three and fourpence, I spent a sleepless night, wondering what Pop would say.

My Guardian Angel must have been working overtime because next morning we went to Ayr races for the Gold Cup, and in a flash of inspiration I remembered that Newmarket stables had a way of 'farming' the northern circuit and put my two shillings each way on a long shot from Jarvis's stable – it won. Following my luck, but with greater caution, I ventured two shillings on the second favourite in the next race. Success. And at the end of the afternoon with three pounds now safely in my grip, I saw a horse go down to the start for the last race like an express train. I was standing near a wonderful-looking bookmaker, wearing a Scotch bonnet with an eagle's feather stuck in it and a ferocious expression. Come on, something said to me, have a go. 'Please may I have five shillings each way on My Birthday?' I asked nervously.

'That'll win nothing,' he said, 'I'll give you 25 to 1, lassie.'

'Right,' I said, clutching my first ever bookie's ticket from J. John in a trembling hand. My Birthday came storming back, winning by five lengths. I was solvent and much more. I had also begun to bet with J. John, the great Scottish bookie, with whom I had an account for many years. Even my silly little bets did not seem to worry him. He always remembered offering me 25 to 1 on My Birthday and how thrilled I had been with that windfall.

One day the same year I met a lady who turned to me as from a great height and asked: 'What are you going to do when you grow up?' Without even pausing to think, and goodness knows why, I replied: 'I am going to be a journalist.' This is only recorded because the very first article I wrote on that same day was bought by *Harper's Bazaar* for three guineas: it was called 'Thoroughbred'. The first sentence read: 'Horse is not a noble animal.'

Early in 1937 I began full-time work for the National Magazine Company and as I walked towards my first office it seemed as if the stars were well placed in the sky, because there was a bookie on the same landing. When the Lincoln (the first big flat race of the year) came along, so did my third winning dream which told me to back Marmaduke Jinks, who obliged at a very long price (what a beauty). This was a good omen, but now began many years of 'Saturdays only' racing, apart from a few wonderful weeks in Ireland before the war.

1937 seemed endless, but a second visit to the Derby came out of the blue. Although I was working, I was still called upon to help find partners to take my younger sister, Daphne, to the endless debutante dances of the era. Having been around for two years already, it was assumed that I knew enough young gentlemen to fill the Albert Hall, and again and again I found myself writing the same pompous note: 'My mother is taking a dinner party to the A's dance on . . . and would be so pleased if you could join her on this occasion.' Once, in desperation, I wrote in a great hurry on office paper to a friend called Francis Williams at Trinity College, Oxford and was surprised to get no answer. Someone else must have been rustled up for the dance, I suppose, but a month or so later my office telephone rang and a very nice voice asked for me. 'I am Francis Williams, but your friend is I expect at Trinity, Cambridge – they sent the letter on to me and it's taken ages to get here. Was it a good party?' We had a giggly conversation which ended in an invitation to lunch – appropriately enough at the Oxford and Cambridge Club.

'But how will I recognize you?' I asked. In the end he agreed to wear a bus ticket in his button-hole if I wore a pink carnation on my coat. It was the greatest fun and Francis Williams the second told me his father-in-law was one of the leading trainers of the day. When he heard of my passion for racing/Peter Thrale, he asked if I was going to the Derby. I explained that my family had no racing interests and I was working, etc. etc. But he said: 'Look, my wife won't be going this year, so why don't you get the day off and come in my father-in-law's box?' So I went to the Derby in the grandest style with champagne as well and half-a-crown each way on the winner at a most unrewarding price. Since then, I have watched from the starting gate with the Thrale family, from a bus with the Garrick Club outing and from the Regent's Stand; but for me the Derby is an event, a jamboree, an outing, a spectacle and a performance only remotely to do with my kind of racing and, from now on, television is the best box from which to watch this marvellous contest.

By this time I was selling advertising and making £5 a week, plus commission. One lucky month netted me twelve pages from a client, which meant quite a substantial success, so I decided to spend the proceeds in advance on a fortnight's holiday in Ireland, only to find that the twelve-page client had gone bust meanwhile. It took a lot of half-crown bets to recoup that little disaster.

The war clouds seemed to loom darker and darker as the months went by, and I went to stay with Helen and her husband Lionel in the Midland Hotel in Manchester for the last pre-war November Handicap. It was lovely to meet Peter Thrale there again and we talked about my hope of owning a horse, knowing that it was impossible, but he asked if I would be able to look after a racehorse for him if war broke out.

In the summer of 1940, a very nice dark brown three-year-old arrived at Yester. I was recovering from an eye infection there after measles, which had meant my leaving London and any work that entailed reading. What an ironical situation to be riding a thoroughbred filly, already the winner of two races, with no hope of seeing her on the racecourse.

I had no idea how fast a horse galloped on the flat, and one day Disobedience, who was very fit, pricked up her ears as we walked into a vast stubble field and I nearly got left behind. When I shortened the reins she was off like a rocket. After that I took care to be more tactful when we reached wide-open spaces. Racehorses are trained to jump off from a standstill and will pull your arms out if you let them, but Dizzy was so amenable that we were soon able to go anywhere without any fuss.

Not long after Dizzy's arrival, my mother suddenly decided that horse transport was in. The inadequacy of Merrylegs, now in her late twenties, as the only candidate was fairly obvious – and a series of ghastly mistakes began. An expert friend of a friend who had once lived in Leicestershire was asked to find a very quiet pony, big and strong enough to pull a useful trap and for lightweight grown-ups to ride. She found him.

I rode five miles to Haddington station to fetch this paragon from Leicestershire one fine morning, lolloping happily along the grass verges on Disobedience. The paragon emerged rather untidily from the railway horse-box, scattering three small boys, a fox terrier and the oldest inhabitant, who had materialized to join the excitement. Then came a nasty sinking feeling – the pony was a strong, bold grey, good-looking enough, but it was either upset by the journey or quite unused to traffic. Disobedience took an instant dislike to it, on being snapped at as we set off for home, leading the newcomer on a very tight rein down the High Street. I was soon scarlet in the face and, by the time we got back two hours later, in a rage. The pony dived towards the hedge whenever a car came into view, and I had to walk most of the way sandwiched between Disobedience, trying to keep up with her long graceful strides, and the pony which jogged, bounced or slithered about like an eel, snatching at bites of grass when it wasn't trying to get away. Mummy was waiting anxiously to see her new (and expensive) asset and she was most annoyed when I said it was hopeless in traffic and not at all quiet.

'Absolute nonsense,' she said, 'it is sold as quiet to ride and drive. You always think you're the only one who knows about horses. Put it in the stable and we'll try it in harness tomorrow.' Once Mummy decided on a course of action, nothing on earth would persuade her to change her mind. I was told to leave the whole thing to the expert, who was arriving in person that night to stay for a week.

When she arrived it did not take me long to establish that the grey pony was (1) Not the pony advertised as quiet to ride and drive; (2) Not the pony Mummy had been negotiating for; (3) Not the pony the expert had really meant to provide, but another just as good. Last, and most important, the expert felt sure the pony would be ideal because it had been thoroughly recommended by a personal friend, although she had never actually ridden it. I was at the stables when the harnessing of the new pony began — and noted its look of sheer amazement when the expert tried to put the collar over its head. It was finally decided to let it wear traces instead — so much easier with a new pony at first. After another little argument about procedure, I felt I must intervene again. I was now absolutely sure the pony had never been near a cart in its life — whenever the expert invited it to back into the shafts, it whipped round, snorting wildly. 'Shut up, Georgina, and mind your own business.' By then the gardener, who was wonderful with horses, had joined the party and he quietly helped to fasten the traces to the cart, while everyone else patted the pony. Then the expert said: 'That's fine, I knew he'd be all right once he settled down,' and unwisely urged the animal forward. The cart of course came too. At which all hell was let loose, and in five pregnant minutes the pony systematically kicked the front of the cart to pieces which seemed to give it great pleasure.

This disaster was rapidly compensated for by a kind friend, Eric, who rushed to an auction at the Elephant and Castle where he bought a 'charming little pony and cart with all the harness', as a present for Mummy. The dangers of buying horses at auction are infinite, unless you are lucky enough to know the animal of your choice personally — to know not only its history, its virtues (if any), but also the disadvantages that have prompted the owners to part with it. Soon two of us were taking the familiar road to Haddington on horseback — the idea was that one person would drive the new pony in its cart, while the other led the spare horse back. At the station we found a beautiful young skewbald stallion in the centre of an admiring crowd — with him was a peculiar high hackney exhibitor's show cart (rather like a water boatman on wheels) with room for one person perched up on a little seat — but there was no harness, just a weird, unrelated selection of straps — no reins — no collar — so we left the cart behind and set off, only to find that the pony was terrified of traffic. It took us all our time to get him out of the town and onto the main road. My sister and I were speechless with alternate giggles and fury. By the time we got home, Eric, who had so kindly paid £120 for the pony and trap, was waiting on the doorstep to greet us. We explained about the pony cart and of course (1) It wasn't the cart he had bought; (2) It wasn't the harness he had seen; (3) He had not realized the pony was only two years old and a stallion at that.

I flatly refused to have anything further to do with the creature and was told angrily by Mummy that, apart from fetching it, no one had asked me to do anything about the pony; so I handed the leading rein to Eric and cantered off to put Disobedience away for the night.

Eric had an awful time getting the pony to the stables, which were about a quarter of a mile away, because it wanted to eat the lovely grass, then it tried to roll on the lovely grass and then it wanted to get away on its own to enjoy the countryside. The pony was in fact unbroken – next day when they managed to harness him to the newly repaired cart, he kicked it to pieces in record time.

Life in Scotland changed dramatically for me on Midsummer Day 1941, when I first met, very briefly, a tall, slim Officer in the Irish Guards. We met twice more and I married Arthur Coleridge. This was a great relief to our village blacksmith, who considered it strange that I had remained unwed whereas my younger sister, Daphne, had dashed off to the altar in true Gretna Green spirit at the age of nineteen. Here I was, already twenty-five, still at large. One day I rode Disobedience down to the forge with my always untidy hair tied back with a ribbon. 'Well, Georgeen,' he said, 'I see you're wearing the green ribbon.' This remark conveyed nothing to me, as I asked Pop what it could have meant, at which he nearly swallowed his after-lunch cigar. Evidently wearing the green ribbon was a clear sign locally of being left on the branch, the shelf, or wherever maiden ladies were filed. I chose another colour hurriedly but, following my gambling instincts perhaps, promised to marry Arthur the first time we were alone together, after meeting him three times in all. My mother was one hundred per cent flabbergasted by this hasty decision. As it happened, no one in the family had seen

Arthur before. He and I mutually and simultaneously proved that there is such a thing as love at first sight. Pop's reaction was typical. He was having his afternoon nap when we arrived, hand in hand, to break the news.

'Well,' he said to Arthur, 'you do realize she hasn't got any money?'

'Neither have I,' said Arthur, 'so that makes two of us.'

We have spent the last thirty-six years proving that it is perfectly possible to marry in haste and to be happy ever after.

3

A Nod is as Good as a Blink

Racing people have a racing face with hat to match, perched at a particular racing angle, a racing walk and a purposeful expression. They tend to form themselves into little purposeful groups which cannot be penetrated by the uninitiated because on the racecourse all is secret – information is whispered, nodded, winked or just withheld. Unsolicited tips, especially from owners, turn out to be the most expensive and should usually be ignored. The day you do ignore an unsolicited tip – fear not, it will turn up at 20 to 1 – but that's racing.

The racing faces have not changed over the years, but attitudes and arrangements for the comparative comfort of racegoers certainly have. Before the war, the idea of a woman riding at a race meeting was quite out of the question (although there were ladies' races at point-to-points) and until 1966 there were no women trainers. A woman could only run a training stable through a man who held the licence in his name, but those barriers have disappeared and there are quite a number of successful women trainers now, and in 1977 a woman rode in the Grand National.

In those days nearly every head wore a hat in the members' enclosure, the men wore bowlers at all times unless there was a heatwave, when panamas popped out shyly, looking rather dashing – if a little yellow at the edges. At country race meetings, brown felt hats also appeared, and 'fast' young men wore long-since forgotten pork-pie hats, which suited hardly anyone and which unfortunately sometimes adorned the heads of maiden aunts who bred golden retrievers. No well-dressed woman ever tied a scarf over her carefully waved hair. The bowler is now almost as rare as the pork pie, and looks particularly odd stuck on top of long, straggly hair. (I was relieved to discover on my marriage that my husband had never owned either a bowler or a pork pie, but these virtues were nearly cancelled out by his affection for a terrible tweed 'Farmer Giles' cap'.) However, in the Royal Enclosure at Ascot morning dress for men is still necessary and women must wear hats, as they did the first time I was taken to the Royal Meeting after being presented at Court, which was an exceptionally shy-making performance.

Way back in the 1930s mothers and daughters in flocks arrived by car to park, nose to tail, in the Mall, waiting to drive into the courtyard. Everyone was dressed in white with a headdress of three white ostrich feathers and full-length white gloves. The presentation was a most embarrassing ordeal, during which I shot past throne one, hurried, curtseying, to the space between it and throne two, curtseying again frantically just past throne two and managing by a miracle not to trip over my dress – Mummy having confiscated my spectacles on the grounds that people did not wear them. She gave me a beautiful little silver lorgnette with a lalique glass cover, but did not understand that the lens had to fit one's particular needs, so however much I stared, I saw very little. In any case there is no way to hold a lorgnette while clutching an evening bag and a large ostrich-feather fan, unless you have three hands.

. . . . .

The applications for Royal Enclosure badges had to be sent to St James's Palace a long time ahead, but any spare time available was spent going through agonies of indecision about what to wear on which day at Ascot.

Getting ready for the Royal Meeting then was quite a performance, requiring four different dresses and four different hats with appropriate shoes, in varying degrees of grandeur. These were discussed over and over again, chosen after endless changes of mind and finally fitted at least twice. Tuesday at Ascot was regarded as not being very smart, Wednesday and Thursday very grand indeed, but Friday was frankly ordinary, for some mysterious reason it was always much more informal. (In 1977 children were allowed in the Royal Enclosure on the Friday for the first time.) 'They' did not always bother to go on the Friday. Who 'they' were was not explained, but 'they' seemed to matter and it was crystal-clear to me that I was not destined to penetrate their circles.

To complete the correct Ascot rig, white or cream-coloured elbow-length gloves, with beastly little buttons which kept popping open, had to be worn all the time. The arguments and anxieties about who should wear what on which day occupied several weeks and blighted the whole prospect. So did my first experience of a race meeting where people strolled aimlessly about the lawn, taking no interest whatever in the horses. Mummy would not walk to the paddock, and I could only see the races if she was so busy talking to friends that she did not notice my spectacles. We paraded about, pausing every few minutes to talk to other couples with daughters in tow; the man would raise his grey top hat, while the woman usually stared enviously at Mummy's elegant clothes and I glared sulkily at the other girls. Some of the women wore diamond bracelets over their long white gloves, and wet white make-up on their faces, under unmanageable picture hats, laden with artificial flowers, fruit and osprey feathers – or a mixture of all three. I thought they were priceless.

My return to Royal Ascot after the war was made even more exciting because I was given a lady's badge for the Jockey Club Stand for the first and only time – and went to watch the Gold Cup from there, thinking it would be much less crowded. I nipped up the stairs and out onto the balcony to admire the beautiful view and was just about to thank my hostess, who was standing nearby, when a very grand lady tapped me on the shoulder and said: 'I do not believe that you are the wife or the daughter of a member of the Jockey Club.'

'No,' I said, 'I was invited here and . . .'

'Well,' she cut me off, 'not here. Your badge is for the floor above.' So I fled, scarlet in the face, to the safer climate higher up, where incidentally, the view was even better. This same lady turned up one Saturday at Hurst Park where she recognized me, and complained that her horse would have won but the jockey had lost both pedals at the start.

'That, my dear,' she kindly explained, 'is what we call the stirrups.' How Peter laughed.

Oddly enough, the special language of the racing fraternity has not changed in forty years. You still canter upsides – slip along a bit – take a strong hold – go like the clappers – or as slow as a church. It is just the same and so are the anomalies – the little pen reserved for the Ladies of the Jockey Club at Newbury – the wooden seats with the owner's name painted on at Cheltenham, on which I once sat down (only once, I assure you). It is the only sport with such a rigid hierarchy; perhaps a strength, perhaps a weakness. Only history will tell.

My post-war Ascot day must have been pretty successful financially; I wrote the names of three winners on my race card and stuck it in our scrapbook for the 1940–1950 decade. With it is a footnote: 'Wot price M'sieur l'Amiral?' George, the hall porter at the Ritz who always knew if one was short of money, had told me to risk five shillings each way on the Aga Khan's horse in the Cesarewitch, when it had won at a very long price indeed – most comforting. Oddly enough, there are hardly any references to racing in this first scrapbook, but in volume three, which is up-to-date, some pages are almost entirely devoted to our racecourse adventures.

Going round Peter Thrale's stables near Epsom where he started training again after the war, was just like old times. He still carried the same favourite walking-stick with a round top for the horses to nibble at, making typical comments in his low, husky voice: 'This is my friend, 100 to 6 last week' – 'That one's no good – silly sort of horse' – 'This old villain can go a bit, but he thinks too much' – 'Here's a nice two-year-old – next Saturday – Hurst Park – you'd better come along.' We went to see the Thrales as often as possible, and I longed more than ever to have a racehorse in training, but as we were only just starting to make our way in London there wasn't a hope. Peter knew how much I wanted a racehorse and we talked it over, agreeing that it was out of the question. I was working in London for Country Life Limited for four guineas a week (part time).

I loved to meet him at Hurst Park on Saturdays. Peter and his son-in-law, the jockey Ken Gethin, won quite a number of races there. Travelling by the race train to Hampton Court was hectic, because one had to share a taxi to the racecourse with as many people as possible (for economy's sake). Some drivers allowed six people to cram in, which was cheap but rather too cosy for comfort in the summer. I made a lot of racecourse acquaintances that way – we never exchanged names, but for several years I watched the racing from a particular place on the stand with a delightful man who sometimes provided useful tips. We believed that we brought each other luck. I hope he still enjoys his racing, although Hurst Park disappeared years ago under rows of houses. To save money, I always took my lunch – a cheese sandwich wrapped in foil, a hardboiled egg and an apple.

Peter very often left a badge for me at the entrance and I met Mrs Thrale and their daughters near the paddock to hear what was 'expected'. Peter never said a horse would win, he would just smile impishly and say: 'Yes, you can risk two shillings.' Usually Mrs Thrale knew precisely what was confidently 'expected'; in that case my whole one pound maximum sometimes, but not often, went into the melting pot. Peter knew the form of rival Epsom horses, which was helpful. Looking through the card he would say: 'Not today, that one's knocking at the door, next time for him – that's a horrible horse – that one can go a bit.'

The 1950s were good times for Peter as a trainer and he won the Cesarewitch for the second time with Three Cheers, and a nice race at Ascot with Sir Phoenix. It was remarkable how his late years were more and more successful and he became a subject for cartoons on the racing pages. Peter's success meant a lot to me financially and gave great pleasure among my colleagues. It was possible in the early '50s to pay for my subscription to *Raceform* out of my modest investments.

Our daughter Frances (Smith) remembers the fun she had as a little girl 'counting out my handbag' when I got home from the races on a Saturday. While I wallowed in the bath, she hunted for two-shilling pieces and practised her arithmetic adding up the loot. Evidently no losing tickets ever came home with me. She clearly remembers counting a wad of pound notes after a good day at Kempton. She tells me that I used to say: 'That's paid for *Raceform*, that's my railway ticket, that's my badge,' and she cannot recall finding me in the red. This may have been the result of extreme caution when I had so very little to spend and placed only very few bets, mostly on Peter's fancied runners. He had one particularly good season which helped me to finance a trip to Paris, taking Frances over. We had a lovely time on the proceeds of my little gambles.

One day Arthur and I went to have lunch with the Thrales. We arrived while Peter was in the middle of a difficult telephone conversation. He rang off, grinning wickedly.
'That's old Smith, he wanted to send me a two-year-old, but I don't want him anywhere near me – he's a boring blighter – doesn't pay his bills – he kept saying "but Peter, she's very well bred", so in the end I said, "so are you, and you're no damn good either."'
At lunch I mentioned a talkative young woman who tended to turn up at race meetings and button-hole the Thrales to get tips. 'No,' he said, 'I haven't suffered from her lately, the only thing to do with a girl like that is to put her in a seller at Newton Abbot.' Peter liked to tease my husband about marrying me for my four guineas a week and gave me great pleasure when he told his friends that I was one of his children, and that he had brought me up. This had started when I was fifteen, when I woke up one morning conscious with black despair that on the next day my fate would drag me to Leatherhead to sit the School Certificate exam, which I had no hope of passing as my maths were non-existent. In a fearful state of misery I rode off to meet Peter, determined to borrow enough money to get me to Scotland where I planned to stay with Dr Martine. Peter listened to my outpourings in silence as we ambled up to the gallops. Then all he said was: 'What time do you have to be at Leatherhead?'
'Nine.'

'Right, wait outside on the road at half past eight and I'll take you.' Not another word was said on the subject. I told my father that Mr Thrale would give me a lift because he was going to Leatherhead in the morning and, as usual, Pop did not comment. True to form, I failed in all three mathematical subjects – so failed the exam, but managed to get away with enough A's in French, Divinity (that was a long shot), English, history and drawing to heal the wounds. Peter had stopped me from refusing at the first fence. Most important, I think this must have been the first bond in our long friendship.

Peter was suitably impressed (with a sly look at Arthur) when I told him in 1949 that I had been offered the Editorship of *Homes and Gardens* at a salary which seemed princely – £900 a year, rising to £1,000 after six months. For a time there was a danger of work seriously impeding my racing, but luckily my secretary's brother was a bookie, so my half-crown each way was easy to place and we had a great time poring over the midday *Standard* every day before lunch. Arthur much preferred cricket, and as I went to catch the race train he would set out for Lord's, sometimes lending me his race glasses because I had none of my own. (A few years ago he gave me a beautiful pair of Zeiss binoculars and liked them so much that he bought a slightly bigger pair for himself.) Occasionally I went in Heygate's bus – which left from Lowndes Square and was organized by a group of race-goers who ran it during petrol rationing. They could nominate a friend if there was a spare seat and (for 12/6 to courses near London) I sometimes joined the party. The first time I travelled in the bus, no one spoke to me all the way there and all the way back, but after two or three ventures into this unknown world I met Mrs Heygate and we became friends.

. . . . .

One Saturday I was carrying home my shopping basket with my daughter, when I stopped to cross the road beside a fellow shopper, who lived a few doors away. She smiled at me and said: 'I must hurry up, we are going to Hurst Park at eleven.'

'Do you go often?' I asked.

'Oh yes,' she said, 'my husband runs *Raceform*, we go every Saturday.' After about half a split second (she tells me) I said: 'Would you ever be able to give me a lift?' We have been going to the races together ever since.

It was a treat to go racing with experts, to hear their sometimes caustic comments about trainers, jockeys, horses, to hear what was supposed to be going to win and which horse they were going to back, although betting was not their main interest. They were publishers first and foremost, but a nice win at a nice price was always welcome. *Raceform* is an accurate week by week record of every race meeting in Britain, with important meetings in Ireland and France as well. In it you can look up the record of every horse that has run up to the week in question. It used to arrive by post in loose sheets to be slipped into a special navy blue binder with 'bootlace' ties. My daughter always did this for me, her fingers being more suitable than mine for the job. Later, *Raceform* became a weekly book (now only the edition by post remains, I shall miss buying the handy little book just when I need it – but that's racing. I am too mean to pay £60 a year for the subscription).

The new stand at Ascot attracted me so much that I became an 'alternative member', under a clever system which gave one a badge and a car park badge for £10 a year (in 1977 – £15 a year), then you paid £1 more at the gate for each day's racing, excluding the Royal Meeting. This is ideal for people who cannot get away very often. Years later Arthur became a member too, so he bought me an ordinary lady's badge. I have never got over my irritation when the over-dressed (some anyway) spectators at the Royal Meeting still stand with their backs to the racecourse, gossiping, while the best horses in Europe are galloping their hearts out.

We next decided to become members at Sandown and Kempton, then Arthur joined Newbury which is by far his favourite racecourse. I prefer York, with Ascot and Kempton next. For the last ten years we have been 'collecting' racecourses, arranging part of our annual holiday to take in a new race meeting. Up to date we have ranged as far as Ayr and Carlisle in the north-west, Devon and Exeter and Ludlow in the south-west. Racecourse officials are almost all helpful and welcoming to strangers. They are proud of their racecourse and often ask us if we have enjoyed ourselves as we leave, especially in the north where everyone is so relaxed and friendly.

Every race meeting has a distinct personality. I suppose Wye in Kent was the least attractive (it has closed) and Pontefract in Yorkshire the nicest surprise. It is so neat, so accessible, set in an oasis of parkland among the slag-heaps. Newcastle has a beautiful racecourse, with a very comfortable grandstand. We stayed at a hotel next door and simply walked through the garden gate, along a wooded lane, a few hundred yards to the Members' Enclosure. On a Monday there was plenty of room and we were very lucky, both managing to win our badge money.

This certainly did not happen when we visited Ludlow in Shropshire. The highly individual layout on the edge of a sandy common, rather like a golf course (perhaps it is a golf course) makes racing hazardous and in one race the field split into rival factions, some riders choosing to go off onto the 'fairway' while the others virtuously followed the more usual track. In the very next race, a loose horse ended up in one of the sandy hollows, or was it a bunker?

On the whole, we loved our day at Ludlow, where I watched a very small horse walking round, led by a very tall man, and wondered, because the horse was twelve years old and running in a hurdle race for the first time, which was strange enough. I very nearly ventured 30p and wish I had. He was the outsider of the party and won – going on to win another five races off the reel. We had seen the debut of Golden Batman, a remarkable little horse which had won many point-to-points and once again proved that winners come in all shapes and sizes.

Wolverhampton was very puzzling – first find your way to the racecourse. We couldn't. Round and round the maze of streets we drove in a most unlikely part of the town, staring at the map and getting rather giggly as we hunted for our target; asking the way from various even more unlikely inhabitants, most of whom appeared not to know that there was a racecourse, until at last we found a charabanc driver who was sure he knew the way: 'Take the fifth turning on the right, then bear left and left again – you can't miss it,' he said.

We missed it all right and found ourselves first facing a blank wall, then the main road to Birmingham, but a timely call at a newspaper shop put us on the right track at last. We arrived to find the car park full, but with the craftiness of desperation, I spoke to a charming official and explained how far we had come and the problems we had faced on this first visit to his racecourse. He very kindly allowed us to leave the car just there, at the entrance, in the only remaining gap.

The spectators vary just as much as the racecourses. Newbury, a very well designed course where every inch of the running can be seen, brings out a rash of meringue-shaped straw hats in the summer, all in brilliant colours, worn at a determined angle on grey heads. The winter changes them into round, brilliant-coloured, bun-shaped felt creations, with a few tea-cosy-like berets and some spectacular fur 'bombs', plus the eternal headscarf, which has moved in everywhere. Nowadays, literally anything goes and almost anything can happen in the Members' Enclosure.

Chepstow is in a hilly wooded setting; it is a charming place on a sunny day. One Easter we watched a family scene develop there between mother, grandmother, small girl and little boy in pushchair. As the mother stood admiring the beautiful scenery, enjoying the sunshine, the little boy kicked off his shoes. While Granny helped her to put them on his wriggling feet again, the little girl attacked a neatly poised row of deck chairs, and pushed them sideways so that they fell like a pack of cards. At which mother and grandmother rushed to capture the girl to make her straighten up the chairs, so the little boy quietly kicked off his shoes again. His mother bent down once more to put them on, at which the little girl dashed off to attack a second row (admittedly this was a lovely game), hotly pursued by grandmother. Then, like a flash, the girl ran away into Tattersalls where she was recaptured after a struggle. For a minute or two peace reigned, after the children had been told a few home truths, then the two ladies, now very hot and thirsty, went to fetch drinks from the bar. At once the little girl darted off again, and her dear little brother undid his harness, wriggled out of the chair like an eel and belted after her. At this point the ladies reappeared, each carrying two cartons of tea, and in their turn dashed off into Tattersalls, waving their arms wildly.

We were laughing at this pantomime, when a more sedate picture developed. It was fascinating to see a neatly dressed lady unpack a large carrier bag on a wooden bench and carefully spread a three-course lunch, with half a bottle of wine, all round her. First she unveiled an avocado pear, with vinaigrette in a plastic bottle, next a plate of chicken salad with mayonnaise and finally a carton of yoghourt. She then proceeded to enjoy the day to the full. The only thing that distracted her attention was a lady on the next bench who was having trouble with her knitting. We felt acutely conscious of the lack of imagination displayed by the cheese sandwiches we were munching. For us, arriving early has always been part of the fun.

Our introduction to Fontwell Park (jumping only) near Chichester was only memorable because our arrival was abruptly interrupted by a car park attendant telling us to take the car away and drive in by the correct entrance. We had made the mistake of driving into the Members' Car Park intending to buy a daily Member's Badge in the ordinary way. It is the only daunting reception we have yet experienced.

When the Racegoers' Club was founded, I joined it at once, and went with the members to the Cheltenham Gold Cup in a charabanc, which was a marvellous day out – beautifully organized. I have only been to this superb meeting twice, the other time was with Dorothy Laird who invited me to go down on the race train with a Press pass. I even watched from the Press Box which has the best possible view, and thoroughly enjoyed hearing informed and caustic comments during every race.

Cheltenham is an ideal steeplechasing course, beautifully sited. It is hard on the horses – it takes the best to win there – but provides a very fine spectacle indeed, even if it gets terribly crowded on the three March Festival days, where nearly every race brings out the champions. It is a tweedy, leather and fur-coated public, dedicated to the world of hunting, point-to-points and the 'winter game', with the county gentry in their ancient, well-cut suits, their wives wearing sensible felt hats and sensible flat-heeled leather boots. There is a definite Cheltenham look that goes with the wooden garden seats in the enclosure which bear the name of their owner painted in big white lettering and are not for sitting on by you and me. I made that mistake remember, that very crowded day, by subsiding onto the only empty bench, but was very soon reminded that this was no common or garden bench, but an exclusive repository for Mrs ... whose name was clearly to be seen written on it – oh dear, but how delightful really.

That day Crisp, a huge, angular-looking horse, who had arrived from Australia, came to Cheltenham with a great reputation. His appearance in the paddock caused a ripple of amazement. He was very tall and gaunt, with every hair standing on end in the cold March wind, giving him a peculiar shaggy rug look. His lop ears and high bony withers all added up to a most unorthodox whole. However, Dorothy Laird had told me about this good horse and on seeing him walk round the paddock with long, sweeping strides, I took a wild plunge and risked 30p each way. He won easily at 9 to 1 and I don't suppose he started at such long odds again, till he ran second in the Grand National to Red Rum. Crisp was a most remarkable animal – one of the very best. (I backed Red Rum in 1977 too, what a beauty!)

The weather can be really cruel at Cheltenham and they certainly got the worst of it there last spring. We soon discovered that however many layers of wool you start out in, an extra jersey should always be at the ready, because it's sure to be much colder than you expect. Nearly every racecourse is bleak, wide open to the four winds, and the stands seem fated to look due north, if not north-east where the icy blast is born. Even my weatherproofing layers of fat have to be supplemented by long woollen stockings (a Christmas present from the grandchildren), high boots with sheepskin socks, long Johns, a woollen dress with a woollen jersey and on top of all that a coat like a horse blanket. On a bad day that's only just enough.

The bookies have an uncanny talent for knowing when it is going to rain, and before a single drop has fallen, the first of many colourful umbrellas flowers in the silver ring. In a matter of seconds, a rash of bright mushrooms has sprouted and the rain begins. It pays to notice these things in good time, because if you have left your umbrella miles away in the car, or in the cloakroom as I invariably seem to do, the bookies' warning can keep you a little less wet.

In 1970 our racing experience was changed as if by magic after a visit to my sister Frances in Sussex.

4

Shutting the Stable Door

Few owners are lucky enough to start a racing career with a horse as brave, as full of character and as successful as Islay Mist. He came into my life almost by accident, and changed the pattern of our existence dramatically. In 1968 my youngest sister, Frances, and her husband, Nigel Pearson, lived on the edge of Ashdown Forest in Sussex, near Chelwood Gate, where they bred Welsh Mountain ponies and she went hunting regularly with the local foxhounds: at meets she often admired a very good-looking thoroughbred mare and one day jokingly suggested to her owner that if ever Footstool had a foal, this would make a perfect replacement for Frances's ageing hunter.

Unfortunately, when the foal was born, Frances had too many ponies to look after so the idea had to be forgotten. Two years later, to her surprise, she was offered the horse 'for a good home' at the bargain price of £250. Although at first sight Islay Mist was not very impressive, Nigel liked him and they decided not to miss this second chance. We often drove down to see them on Sundays, and when I rang up to make a date Frances said she had a new toy to show me. I thought there must be a new pony (there were usually a dozen mares and foals for me to admire, and I invariably compared them one by one with Merrylegs, automatically taking it for granted that there could never be any comparison with Foalie).

We arrived on a fine winter's day to find Frances looking very mysterious. She wasted no time, but hurried me from the car straight into the nearest field where, towering over the ponies, on the skyline, there was an awkward-looking, gawky, giraffe-like brown horse.

'That's Willy,' said Frances proudly, 'he's going to be my hunter. He's very well bred.' I thought she must have made a ghastly mistake, but just as I was about to make a really sisterly remark about the creature's conformation, Islay Mist (stable name Willy) turned and strode majestically towards us, as if the world was at his feet.

And my mad idea was born.

'He's very well bred,' said Frances again, 'but I can't find the bit of paper. He's registered as Islay Mist.'

Don't ask me why, I still don't know what made me so sure about that horse — impulse, instinct, whatever it was, nothing would have stopped me. My sister and I stared at each other, then I said:

'Have you thought of putting him in training?'

'I thought you'd say that,' she answered, 'but we don't know a trainer any more and he's really my hunter.'

My pulse was racing by now, I could hardly believe in this stroke of luck. A few minutes later, Arthur and Nigel joined us to watch Willy walk into the stables.

'That horse looks as if it ought to be on the racecourse,' said Arthur to my astonishment. He had only recently become interested in racing, but noticed at once that Willy had something special; a beautiful head, and a definite look about him. Perhaps there was a potential racehorse in the family. What next?

Once before, nearly twenty years ago, Frances owned a very fast thoroughbred mare which she longed to send to

Peter Thrale, but neither of us could possibly afford training bills, so the mare was sold when Frances came to live with us in London before her marriage.

I did not realize how wholeheartedly she shared my ambition, because Frances says very little. Now it was amazing how quickly our plans were laid. Before lunch was over we had agreed to form a partnership, Frances and I, the horse to run in my colours, but to revert to her ownership after his racing career. We would share training bills, but I would be responsible for all the paperwork, registration fees and entries, while Frances took on the insurance.

We had the horse, what about finding a trainer? I promised to find someone near enough to Ashdown Forest so that the Pearsons could see the horse often.

We drove back to London in a fever of delighted excitement. It was so extraordinarily lucky for me just at that moment to have the thrill of thinking about Islay Mist, because I faced a tiresome eyesight problem, which would take me to Moorfields from time to time for the next few years.

That same evening, not losing a moment, I rang up Dorothy Laird, who knows all there is to know about the racing fraternity, to ask who trained hurdlers in Sussex, and who would give us an honest opinion of an unknown quantity like our two-year-old. Dorothy Laird answered at once: 'Miss Auriol Sinclair at Lewes – but she won't train just any horse. A trainer of her standing will only take a horse with obvious potential and if she likes the look of it. You have to be lucky to get into a stable like hers.'

I rang Frances next, to tell her that the ideal racing stable was only nine miles away and that the missing pedigree was now essential. 'That's all right,' said Frances happily, 'I've found it. He's Islay Mist by Same Again by Anwar, out of Footstool by King's Bench by Hyperion.'

Our two-year-old gelding was certainly well enough bred and by an extraordinary coincidence he was one of very few foals sired by Same Again, who was the winner of many hurdle races when he was trained by guess who – Peter Thrale. It was really rather uncanny.

The next move was with me. I wrote to Miss Sinclair, posted the letter, and waited anxiously for the answer. Then, when she kindly agreed to inspect Willy, waited again in even greater excitement for the verdict. For some time I had noticed how well-turned-out Miss Sinclair's charges looked, how fit they were and how well they jumped, so it was wonderful news to hear that she was willing to take Islay Mist on a trial basis, on condition that first we sent him to be broken in by David Barker when he was three.

Willy went off in the spring and came home quiet enough for a lady to ride! Perhaps he was – he did not try to run away or buck, but we heard from David that he had some very awkward quirks which had made him more difficult than usual to break in. For instance, Willy flatly, categorically refused to walk through water. Nothing on earth – shouts, friendly pats, threats, strength – nothing could make him. Finally, he was allowed to walk round rather than upset the other young horses. Willy also disliked tractors. He saw one out of the corner of his eye and stood still, rooted to the spot. Tugs, shouts, taps on the shoulder – nothing moved him. Then one of the stable girls suggested bringing out a young mare so that Willy would follow her past the tractor. The mare was ridden forward, Willy looked at her thoughtfully for a moment or two, then stretched his neck out like a cobra and bit her as hard as he could.

Yet another time it took David Barker two hours to get Willy to walk out of his box. For no apparent reason he would not budge, but just stood there. David waved a stick at him, so Willy snapped it nearly in two. In the end, four people heaved him bodily into the yard. Willy must have been amused by their exertions, he did not kick or struggle – but once outside pawed the ground energetically as if everyone else had been keeping him waiting, and walked on as if nothing had happened.

During this time, Auriol invited us all to see her horses and we drove over to meet the Pearsons at Lewes one Sunday. The Nunnery Stables are tucked away down a steep slope in a side street in quite the most unlikely corner of the town, so I missed the turning three times (earning a low popularity rating as a map reader), and learned a good deal about the traffic systems at Lewes, before finding the entrance.

Twenty years had flown by since the last time Peter took us round his stables and the sight of those long, lean heads peering at us over the loose-box doors, the sound of hay being munched, the clink of hooves, the gentle 'huffles' of welcome for Polomints was almost too nostalgic. I could hardly bear to wait for Islay Mist/Willy to join Auriol's string.

He came back from David Barker, fitter and much sleeker. Frances was asked to lunge him for half an hour (that is to make the horse circle on a long rein, walking or trotting round), then to ride him quietly about the forest for an hour or so every day, to keep him fit until he was old enough to go to Lewes. Nigel worked in London, so there was no one to help during the week; luckily Frances, although small and very slight, is extremely strong on a horse and absolutely fearless. Lunging a horse entails keeping him moving steadily, waving a riding-whip if necessary to stop him coming towards you to pass the time of day. At times, of course, some horses do their best to drag you into the next county. Willy knew all about being lunged and behaved perfectly till one morning he decided that it was far too boring, so he went on strike. He just stood there, head high, ears pricked, gazing out at the misty slopes of Ashdown Forest, while Frances shouted: 'Walk on, Willy', and quite a lot besides. She waved the whip, Willy looked at her amiably, almost pityingly. He was not in the least afraid of whips, no one had ever hit him and I suppose he was as sensible as most three-year-old thoroughbreds. But Willy was on strike. Occasionally he stood up, waving his front legs, still landing in the same place. After a while, Frances decided to ride him instead. No sooner was she in the saddle, than Willy stood up on end like a circus horse, his front legs flailing, going up and down like a lift, again and again. Frances stood this until she thought those wild front feet were getting too near the fence for comfort and jumped off, determined to get Willy going on the lunge – or else.

Frances lunged him for a whole hour, hoping he would be the one who got tired first. Then bravely got back into the saddle for their usual ride. Without warning, Willy went straight up on his hindlegs, but Frances had had enough of it by then, so she raised her right hand ready to slap him hard across his naughty brown ears. At which Willy surrendered and he never tried it again.

He had other maddening habits – Willy ate his rug (very expensive), starting at the nearest mouthful and gradually tearing it to shreds; he ate the edge of the stable door; Nigel's riding gloves; the edge of the manger; the wall; the window frame; in fact he nibbled absolutely anything and everything. Especially people who stopped unwisely to look at his legs – they were rewarded by a swift nip in the seat. Anyone leading him along was nipped in the elbow. Auriol told me, a year later, that she had overheard one of the lads lecturing Islay Mist: 'Now then, Willy,' he was saying, 'you are not to bite Miss Sinclair on the arse.'

Apart from having over-active teeth, Willy was well behaved and although fearfully obstinate at times, he bore no malice and liked people on the whole. After a bit Frances fitted him with a leather collar to stop him murdering his rugs and spent hours dabbing dark brown, sticky stuff with a nasty taste all over the place (including herself by mistake) to stop the nibbling. It was quite a job looking after Willy single-handed and he still objected to puddles, oily patches of tar on the road and specially to wet, muddy places in the forest. Faced with these he would stand snorting, but eventually could be persuaded past, as if treading on broken glass. So the daily ride seldom went by without some sort of battle. The first time he met a fallen branch Willy tapped his front legs hopping over it clumsily. Next time out, Frances was cantering gently along a familiar path when they were faced with two fallen trees. Willy stood off like a steeplechaser and jumped so big that she was nearly left behind. We were delighted to know jumping came so naturally to him.

It had been quite a strain for Frances coping with our young hopeful – which leads me to tell you that there is really nothing noble about the horse, except perhaps its appearance. This is proved conclusively when the creature steps on your toe. Ten to one, as you hop about in agony, a swift nip will remind you that the front end is armed with fangs. I feel bound to point this out in spite of your possibly being the proud owner of an expensive new thoroughbred, just in case your illusions need protecting.

Those limpid, lustrous, equine eyes, so charmingly portrayed in children's books, can turn instantly to blobs of jet black with white edges – a warning signal that mostly comes too late to save the unwary from a neatly aimed kick. These manifestations must all be taken in a purely friendly spirit, because horses are a national symbol of almost every virtue – courage, boldness, hard work, beauty, breeding, elegance, honesty – the lot. St George, Alexander the Great, Princess Anne and Harvey Smith have only horses in common – but the link is as powerful as it is strange, and horses have a peculiarly insidious magnetism. Difficult to explain away and almost irresistible to the mugs, who are being born even more often every minute, if the 1977 yearling sales are any sort of guide.

Why should human beings like horses? They take up a lot of valuable space, make an awful mess which has a particularly persistent, instantly recognizable scent, eat expensive food all day (and all night) and even try to eat while you are trying to ride them. Let your attention stray for a second and down goes that bony head, and before you can grab the reins, he's eating again. Horses drink endless buckets of water too, which have to be filled at regular intervals. Nine out of ten times, the playful creature gives you a nudge in the elbow just at the crucial moment and where does that cold water end up? In your shoes.

The horse has a silky, tangled mane, a long straggly tail, and in winter a thick, scurfy coat – all of which he expects you to keep shiningly clean summer and winter – and does he thank you for it? Think again.

All over Britain, in beautifully arranged airy loose-boxes, thoroughbred horses are waiting, leaning nonchalantly on three hooves, the fourth delicately pointed to show utter relaxation, waiting to be cosseted, expecting to be admired, brushed, combed, massaged, pedicured and coiffured, not once a week, but every damn day; twice if they have been exercised and sweated up a bit (they always sweat).

As the devoted lad/lass/horse person approaches and tries to catch the halter, so thoughtfully stuck on the horse's head to catch it with (first catch your horse), the animal whips round skittishly, presenting a large backside in a threatening manner, reminding you that hindlegs are a powerful defence mechanism, built for lashing out. Remember that the thoroughbred is never evilly disposed — just playful, kittenish, spirited; it is up to human beings to get missed by those steel-shod, pile-driving hind feet.

Your move. Seizing the yard brush firmly, advance into the loose-box shutting the door (no proverb is easier to prove than the one about shutting the stable door after, etc. etc.). Shut it very quickly indeed with you inside and there is a sound even chance that grooming will now take place. Wily horse keepers go in for an endless supply of Polomints — a sweet which seems to excite absolute passion in racehorses, who drool at the sight of the packet and would bite you very hard indeed if you walked past within reach without paying Polomint tribute. Having Polominted yourself into a halter-catching position the scenario improves at once. A horse tied firmly to a steel ring in the wall is much less impressive. He can be brushed, he can be asked to show you the inside of his grubby hooves, to give you the doubtful pleasure of picking them clean with (oddly enough) a hoof-pick. This often used to occur on penknives, scout variety, which were considered very desirable when I was eleven. The horse, when asked to let you examine his front hoof nearside, will usually oblige — but the hind foot is more difficult. It seems to have an extra elastic joint just halfway up the leg, so that just as you notice with a practised eye that a pebble is jammed into the frog (the soft centre) — wham, the hind foot is whipped away and used for standing on again. It's jolly good exercise and blacksmiths thrive on it. Unfortunately horses are furnished with two of these highly sprung back legs, so whatever hard work goes into dealing with leg one, is redoubled when attempting to examine hoof two, because the horse, like you, is getting warmer and more agitato every minute.

Clipping horses is yet another hazard. Sometimes no problem at all, but if the horse is ticklish round the tummy, and many of them are, the fireworks begin. I once left Jane with a beautifully tonsured neck, shoulders, back and just nearly to the tail, after which the kicking and squealing had put a stop to any further clipping. She looked absolutely ridiculous with her stomach covered in fur, a patchy backside and woolly 'gaiters'. It took two days to get the job finished. Now I suppose one would give the horse a tranquillizer – quite a few racehorses are so hysterical about being clipped that they have to be just about anaesthetized.

You can imagine that Frances heaved a sigh of relief when Auriol Sinclair sent the horse-box to fetch Islay Mist in July and another bout of quivering anticipation began – would Willy make the grade?

After the longest four weeks I can remember, a prophetic letter came from Auriol on 30th July 1971: 'I have just written to your sister to tell her that Willy has not eaten his lad or his equipment and to my utter astonishment has not been heard to wind-suck or crib-bite. He is cantering on the peat moss gallops and at this stage I am sure he looks like a racehorse in the making.' At once I wrote to Weatherbys to register Frances and myself as racehorse owners in partnership and started negotiations for a set of racing colours. We also formally registered the authority for Miss A. V. Sinclair to act as our trainer. There was no hope of reviving our great-grandfather's blue and cream, but I finally chose a sky blue jacket with white cross belts and a blue and black hooped cap. All this has to be carefully indicated on a special form and the fee is £2.50 (I believe). The registration of colours must be renewed annually, otherwise it lapses and your colours can be allotted to someone else. Next came a letter from the Registration Department of the Jockey Club, saying that my colours would be registered in the Racing Calendar of 30th September 1971. This was another great moment. Meanwhile, Nigel and Frances insured Willy (at £8% per year).

During this lobbing backwards and forwards of papers (and cheques) without which no racehorse can compete in public, we all met on the chalky downs high above Lewes to see Willy canter one beautiful sunny morning. The old racecourse forms part of the gallops which are shared by the local trainers, but most of the buildings are derelict, apart from an excellent range of boxes which Auriol used to house part of her string. I had last visited Lewes races with Peter Thrale just after the war, so here was yet another slice of nostalgia.

Standing with Frances, Arthur and Nigel waiting for the horses to canter up from the distant hidden slopes, with the sun, the skylarks, the daisies and the scent of gorse, was a glorious escape from the realities of life and work in London. Far below in a deep fold in the downs, there was another gallop which took the horses up a pretty steep hill and on our left the view stretched out to sea. How often we have been there since. It is always very peaceful on the downs, but on cold days the wind might have come straight from Siberia. That first visit showed us a much sleeker, rounder Willy, cantering towards us, quickening slightly as he came past – then trotting back to circle round with the other horses, to be admired. I hardly recognized him, he was puffing like a grampus, but looked well pleased with life, beautifully groomed and shining. Suddenly I realized that this was my first appearance in the unfamiliar rôle of the actual 'owner'. It felt most extraordinary after the many problems of various kinds I had heard trainers discussing and failing to resolve with owners. Here I was in the new rôle of the paying customer, no longer a mere spectator, but a contributing factor – inspecting my property and feeling very happy indeed.

Miss Sinclair turned out to be an even more delightful personality than we had thought after our first meeting, and this new friendship has been the nicest thing that Willy conferred on us all. She was pleased with our horse's progress and with the way Frances had kept him exercised so that he was already far from flabby after only a few weeks in training. Expert feeding, expert grooming, had now begun to improve that gawky frame. Willy was a smallish, neat, but strongly made horse with very good shoulders and powerful quarters. He moved well and was very keen and, up to a point, amenable; just occasionally true to form – he would suddenly stand rooted to the spot, gazing into space until he was good and ready to go. We handed out Polomints, patted Willy and returned to London, already looking forward to our next visit a month later.

By that time, Willy had changed again. He was more muscular, much more grown-up, but still rather small beside the big steeplechasers at exercise with him. He cantered up sharply, pulling very hard indeed with Roger Rowell, Auriol's tall young stable jockey, thoroughly at home on him, sitting easily as they pulled up and came back to circle round us. I thought Roger would look very smart in my blue and white colours, with his fair hair and bright blue eyes. The colour scheme was ideal for our dark brown horse. My colours had actually arrived from Newmarket (£19.50 in 1972 – more by now).

These occasional visits could not disguise the fact that we were waiting, and waiting and waiting. This is the fate of every owner with a young unmade thoroughbred, because it takes months of care, skill and patience to produce a racehorse from soup to nuts. It is an endlessly demanding task which needs a pretty elastic purse to finance it. Generally speaking, the bigger and heavier the horse, the longer you wait. Even our comparatively wiry animal would not be fit enough to run until Christmas.

At last the postman delivered a letter from Lewes containing a new thrill – it announced the first two engagements for Islay Mist/Willy. The great moment was coming closer now. He had been entered on successive days at the Kempton Christmas Meeting in two similar Novice Hurdle races for three-year-olds. I rang Frances to share the excitement, and we were delighted when Auriol chose to run him on Boxing Day.

We all converged on Kempton, bursting with pride at the idea of arriving there as owners. It was the nicest kind of December morning and set a weather precedent, because Willy never once ran in the rain. Even if the weather was unsettled, the sun came out for him every single time. It made racing that much happier when we discovered that he had this special gift. It was most exciting to claim my first owner's badge (owners are each allotted two badges and two free race cards) and to see in the race card:

		Trainer	St	lb
19	ISLAY MIST		10	0
	Br g Same Again – Footstool			
	Lady Georgina Coleridge			
	(Miss A. V. Sinclair, Lewes)	R. Rowell		
	SKY BLUE, WHITE X belts, BLACK			
	and BLUE hooped cap			

Already we had gloated over Saturday's *Sporting Life* where our horse featured among the declarations, but that race card is a precious souvenir. It had been such a very long haul.

. . . . . .

Watching Willy being saddled was a thrilling new experience too, then came the best moment of all as Frances, Nigel, Arthur and I walked into the paddock with our trainer to form one of those close little racing groups. We were the 'connections' so often mentioned by TV commentators.

It felt very peculiar as we stood there waiting for the jockeys to file out of the weighing-room, watching Willy walk round quietly, looking rather small, but fit and muscular. He took a great interest in his surroundings, but did not play up or fuss until Roger — elegant in my virginal mint-condition colours, knitted into a beautiful thick jersey — came to 'get mounted please'. It may have been the announcement that triggered him off, but Willy set another precedent — he stood up on end three times, but after this minor demo, went down to the start all right, and took an undistinguished, but satisfactory part in the race. My colours were ideal to see, even at a great distance.

Willy came back mud-splattered, blowing hard, but unscathed. He had jumped perfectly and he did not finish last. The worst of my worries had melted away. Ever since Frances agreed to let me share her horse for his racing career, I had been afraid he would be injured and this worry accompanied me whenever he ran. Auriol was pleased with Willy's first effort, which she said would bring him on tremendously, so we patted him goodbye and drove home, already looking forward eagerly to the next attempt.

I had arranged to ring Auriol that night to find out if Willy was all right. If a horse eats his supper after a race, there is nothing to worry about — and one asks the same question each time: 'Is he all right, has he eaten up?' He was and he had. But three days later we met our first major reverse. It was a foretaste of those frustrations, disappointments and heartbreaks that lie in wait for racehorse owners; and which are only too often greeted with: 'That's racing.' A singularly unhelpful remark which gets more and more tiresome with repetition. Poor Willy was coughing. He had caught the virus which meant that he could not run again till the end of March. What an anticlimax!

The virus is public enemy number one, it hits good, bad or indifferent horses alike at any time, anywhere, in varying degrees of pestilentialness. It is a thoroughly unpleasant sort of 'flu which can put a horse out of action for months. So can the cough to a lesser degree. This is allied to the virus and you are lucky if your horse just has a plain cough, because it only takes about three weeks to get over this very common, ultra-infectious plague. There are injections to help fight these germs, but it is a very lucky stable that escapes them.

You would hardly believe how many other assorted equine ailments there are knocking about – from colic to ringworm, to warbles, to wolf teeth (the better to nip you with), to blood disorders, to corns – imagine a racehorse with corns. Many of them run as if they had bunions too, but that's beside the point. Horses also suffer from all the usual problems of the athlete. For a start, they have ridiculously thin ankles to support them (and their riders) so this gives them a built-in tendency to strain, pull, nick, chip, fracture or just cut their silly looking legs at the drop of a hay net. Any minute the telephone will ring: 'Sorry, the horse has had a slight setback – nothing much.' Being translated this usually means three weeks.

Islay Mist had got the virus really thoroughly, so he spent the whole of January and February being pampered, gradually coming back into work. At long last a new list of engagements came at the beginning of March, and there we were again, trembling on the brink.

Wye in Kent, on 27th March was to be the venue. As

a race meeting this was just about as humble as you could get. We set off down the A2 in a state of palpitating excitement on a lovely morning. On the way we passed a piebald pony, tail end towards us (very lucky), two magpies (lucky) and, to complete the good omens, a parson with a red beard riding a bicycle — what more could one wish for? However, the racecourse was not easy to find. It is (or was) tucked away from the charming little town behind the railway station. We tracked it down finally, driving down a very narrow road into what seemed to be a farmyard with huge Kentish barns. The course was in a field beyond, so we proudly claimed our owner's badges and waited for Auriol and the Pearsons.

Islay Mist looked even more grown up by now. He was officially a four-year-old (racehorses automatically have their birthdays on 1st January). Three months had given him time to build up into a sleek, muscular creature, his dark spring coat glistening as we watched him being saddled. He always quivered with excitement, standing very still, ears pricked, while Auriol and Mick, the travelling head lad, tightened the girths, fastened leather boots (gaiters to you and me) onto each leg, tested the elastic breast girth and checked the running martingale. He was certainly well equipped. This time, after another brief demo in the paddock, he ran an undistinguished race, pulling very hard, but jumping well, considering that this was only his second public appearance. He came in muddy, hot, blowing a good deal, but intact.

Frances smiling broadly, her big grey eyes sparkling, said: 'I wonder how many duck's eggs we have to collect before he gets into the frame?' We now waited to hear: 'Is he sound, has he eaten up?' All was well, so we began to look forward to the Easter Monday meeting at Plumpton, only a few miles from Lewes, where Willy was entered in yet another Novices' Hurdle.

. . . . .

We set out for Plumpton on a perfectly lovely day, proudly displaying our Car Park label, threading our way through the Sussex lanes in brilliant sunshine. Frances and Nigel would meet us there and we went on ahead to make sure that they would be given complimentary badges too. Frances did not want her name to be on the race card during that first year, so I constantly heard myself explaining that Islay Mist/Willy was only mine, or rather half mine, during his racing career and that we raced him in partnership in my colours. On 3rd April the going was pretty firm, the sun shone and there was a big Easter crowd with plenty of runners to entertain them. There were fourteen in our race, which was the last on the card – a very nerve-racking situation, which intensified as the day wore on. Five whole races to tenterhook our way through – the fifth in fact did not figure in our programme, instead Frances and I dashed off to the stables to watch Willy being saddled up. Again he wore his elastic breast girth (to stop the saddle slipping), a running martingale, crossed nose bands and rubber reins. On such a small horse the effect verged on the comic, and I heard a spectator say that he looked like a Christmas tree. Our horse pulled really hard and had such fixed ideas that restraint was essential. Willy stood still to be saddled, quivering all over with excitement, ears pricked, longing to get on with it. In the paddock he strode round with Colin, the lad who always 'did' him, keenly interested in everything he saw, but behaving perfectly.

By now we had walked into the paddock to form our little group more naturally; it was, after all, the third time. Willy looked sleek, fit and very well indeed. We were comparing him favourably with the opposition when Roger appeared in my elegant blue and white colours and tried to get mounted. At which Willy went berserk, he stood up on end three times, nearly squashing a distinguished trainer, who moved his bowler-hatted head out of the way just in time. Then bouncing about kangaroo-wise, he just gave Roger time to climb on before skeetering out of the paddock in a shower of dust. Willy came past the stands in a series of bounding leaps, which looked most uncomfortable, but arrived safely enough at the start.

At Plumpton, the two-mile hurdle races start on the far side of the car park, so it is not easy to see what is going on unless you are high up on the grandstand. I was too excited to watch with the others, but climbed to what I hoped would be a good vantage point, after venturing £2 each way on the Tote, plus 50p each way for one of my colleagues at the office. Willy was a rank outsider, so the local intelligence service obviously did not rate his chances very highly. Nor did any of us.

'They're under starter's orders. They're off.' Nothing of interest happened until the runners had covered about half a mile, then I saw that my colours were well placed in the middle of the field. When the horses came past us for the first time, I heard: 'Islay Mist has joined the leading group', he was about seventh and still pulling hard. At the top of the hill he had moved into fourth place – 'Islay Mist is making up ground', and at the turn into the straight: 'Islay Mist has joined the leaders.' Then, incredibly: 'Islay Mist has hit the front and is streaking away.' He had won by four lengths.

The surprise and the excitement was so intense that I could hardly get through the crowd to lead him in and even forgot what to say: 'I must fetch the horse,' I muttered, pushing my way frantically towards the rails. Winners at 20 to 1 cause a fearful hush, but in a daze I rushed to meet the victorious Willy, seized him by the bridle and led him smartly in the wrong direction till Roger re-directed me and we ended up at the unsaddling area in front of the stands, to find the delighted smiles of Frances, Auriol, Nigel and Arthur. We had won at

14 to 1 on the Book and 20 to 1 on the Tote – what a beauty!

It had taken me forty-one years to lead in my first winner; no other experience on the racecourse will ever live up to the thrills of that £204 Novice Hurdle. Willy's future now looked most encouraging, perhaps my mad idea was not so mad after all.

5

The Trainer States the Following will not Run

Islay Mist was now so firmly established at Lewes that when we called there to gloat over him one Sunday, Polomints in hand, he wore his name in brass letters on his halter. Willy had indeed arrived. But I was completely in the dark about his prospects, because my Saturday racing near London during the past twenty years had mostly been on the flat, which gave me no inkling as to the strength of the opposition, let alone the difficulty of keeping a hurdler in one piece, or how often he would be able to run.

The racehorse population of this country is over 11,000 strong. Rather more than half run over fences; the others on the flat, and of that well-bred and pampered lot, only a small percentage ever troubles the judge, let alone the photo finish. Quite a few reach the sale ring as yearlings, go into training as two-year-olds and are never heard of again (just as well in a good many cases). Gradually the stars come twinkling out — some are too meteoric to last, others get talked into prominence too soon and disappoint, until by the middle of the season it is possible to pick out the best, or at least that's what you think. Meanwhile, owner after owner awaits the day when the great moment will arrive and he will become a winning statistic. The odds against being one of these are so long that it's worth considering some of the hazards.

You would imagine that a racehorse entered in a nice little race, suited to its talents, might help out by concentrating on getting itself ready like any dedicated athlete. All is set towards one target – everyone making every effort to achieve it. Then the trouble starts. First a dry cough, a snuffle, and another dry cough. In a flash the news spreads – he's coughing. Sometimes this tiresome, catching complaint is not serious, but whatever happens the horse cannot run that week, the next week or even in three weeks, because having caught the beastly cough, he has to get over it. No going out with the string to exercise, just a nice little walk perhaps to nibble the grass on a fine day – lazy brute! He certainly takes his time to recover. After which, he takes his time to get fit after getting over it. All of which is expensive and the next stumbling block can be a change of going, which was ideal when the cough started, but has dried up completely, and is now as hard as a brick.

The most dedicated non-runners develop the habit of going lame *à propos* of nothing at all. They are simply rheumatic and stiff like you and me, but seem determined to dwell on it – hobbling about like elderly uncles/aunts (this is usually shoulder lameness from landing on the far side of a jump with an unpredictable weight on your back – try it sometime, I bet your shoulder would be lame too). Pulling a muscle can happen to absolutely anyone/horse and apart from that, believe it or not, their feet are even more vulnerable than ours, in spite of steel shoes. They have a most extraordinary talent for treading on the one and only flint in the district – bruised foot – ten days' holiday at least.

There is also a trick of getting cast in the box which

means that the silly creatures lie down so awkwardly that they cannot get up again without help — unbelievable. But horses are an awkward shape and make the worst of it — banging themselves against the walls, or spraining precious ligaments in the struggle to get off the floor.

Another big danger: fellow racehorses must never be underestimated. Horses dislike each other just as people do, but display their feelings more violently by lashing out. Sometimes the kick lands harmlessly on the enemy's backside, or in his ribs, but even a slight kick on the shins can spell real trouble. Horses even damage themselves by cracking a bone cantering along a beautifully smooth expanse of age-old turf.

Let me tell you what actually happened during Willy's brief career:

One run — then the virus (three months off);

Next run — trod on a stone (ten days rest);

Due to run at Worcester — ran away down main road — jarred front legs (ten days rest);

Due to run at Kempton — coughing (three weeks off);

Ran at Lingfield — badly bruised foreleg (two months off).

I forgot to mention the risk of spreading a plate (casting a shoe). You must have seen this on TV often enough. It's maddening if it isn't your horse — most embarrassing when it is. The runners are now going down to the start. It is still possible to go lame on the way, or to be kicked as they mill about. How often does a horse flatly, categorically refuse to take part? Well, not too often perhaps, but if it's your horse the disappointment is really only just worse than getting left flat-footed as the others fly away from the tapes.

One can go on alternating between coughing, hard

going, waterlogged racecourses, the virus (this is coughing in spades with nobs on) till the end of the season looms ahead and the hopeful winner is still in his box, resting comfortably and accepting delicious meals offered at regular intervals. He hardly even has to bother to go out for exercise.

Having accepted the unpalatable truth that there are so many possible slips between your horse and the winning post, where and when will it run? In my experience making plans to go racing on a particular date that suits you is a waste of time; wherever you hope to be on day X, the horse will be sent two hundred miles away. I had always meant to be there every time my horse was in action, because there is little point in being owned by the animal unless one can get a little 'fun' out of it, and Islay Mist never ran without us being there to cheer him on.

Entries are made about two weeks beforehand for run of the mill races (for my sort of horse) but important contests, such as the Classics, are a far more serious matter. Entries for these go in nearly eighteen months ahead, in fact it is rather like putting a son down at birth for Eton – or do I mean the MCC? The Classics are a thing apart, with several hundred early entries, gradually melting away as each 'forfeit' stage is reached until, at the last forfeit stage, a reasonable number declare to run.

Each racecourse has a safety limit and if too many horses are entered in minor races these are divided into separate sections. In handicaps there can be a ballot among the horses allotted the lowest weight, to reduce the numbers. Being 'balloted out' is quite outstandingly irritating if your horse happens to be nicely in at a very advantageous place at the bottom of the handicap and 'expected'.

A horse can be withdrawn overnight, but not on the day itself, unless there is a valid reason and we all know what thoroughbreds can think up when it comes to 'The trainer states the following will not run'. Classic horses are guarded like the Crown Jewels, so their last-minute accidents are few, but the cough, a bruised foot, or sore shins can happen to the best.

All entries go to Weatherbys and they vary from the humble Novice Hurdle – £2 to enter, £5 extra if declared to run – to the Derby which costs £25 to enter up till February, plus £50 extra in November, another £25 in April and another £50 in May. With, believe it or not, yet another £250 if you declare the horse to run immediately before the race. This all adds up to £400. One year there were over 700 entries which shrank to 26!

The cost of entries gives a clue to the gulf separating a Derby horse from a Novice Hurdler. They are as different as a cheetah and a pekinese, but the breeding could well be identical. Like you and me, every horse is an individual; unfortunately just like us, there are baddies and goodies among them and it takes time to discover which is which.

One beautiful-looking horse that sold for 42,000 guineas as a yearling and was described as 'attractive, shapely colt', ran eight times on the flat, managing to be second just once and was then sold for £1,200. He has so far won a Novice Hurdle and has been second once – so it is neither the price nor the looks, nor the breeding that can guarantee success. There is really no way to determine excellence in advance. Here is a very rough guide to the pecking order:

Flat Races

Classic Entries
Pattern Race possibilities (part of an international scheme)
Grade 1 Handicappers
Grade 2 Handicappers
Grade 3 Handicappers (there are hundreds of these
   bashing about year after year)

Maiden Two Year Olds (bright and hopeful)
Maiden Three Year Olds (still hoping)
Maiden Four Year Olds (oh dear)
Last come the Selling Platers of all ages.

Hurdle Races

Three Year Old Novice Hurdlers (bright and hopeful)
Four Year Old Novice Hurdlers (straight from the flat)
Four Year Old and upwards Handicap Hurdlers (could be very good)
Five and Six Year Old Novice Hurdlers (oh dear me, but they have races for these too)
And Selling Platers of all ages (pretty shopworn by now)

In a Seller, every runner can be 'claimed', that is, bought for the price listed in the conditions of the race and the winner is always auctioned immediately after the race (if anyone is brave enough to bid for these not always totally desirable animals).

A Maiden is a horse which has never won a race, and just to confuse you a Novice is too – but if you want further clarification, all the rules of racing are in *Ruff's Guide* which is beautifully explicit and among other essential facts tells us that: 'Winner means the winner of a race.'

A very competitive group of Hurdlers consists of recent castaways from flat racing, who were already fairly successful and they can now come into their own in handicaps, where the prize money is considerable. At the top of the tree is the Champion Hurdle at Cheltenham.

Islay Mist was a four-year-old Novice Hurdler and my ambitions for him were extremely vague. I simply wanted to see the horse run well and pull up sound. His win had been such a wonderful surprise that it took ages to get over the excitement. The lesson I now learnt most forcibly is that owners must develop a special variety of obstinate patience. After his triumphant Easter, Islay Mist went back to race at Wye, and this time he was (big deal) a 'selection' in the newspapers. Willy was in sparkling form. He left the paddock at great speed in a series of cat-like bounds and leaps, but in the race kept fighting his way to the front, so that he ran out of steam by the finish. He was fourth; this was a great disappointment, but the sun had shone, the horse had jumped like a stag; so with unflagging enthusiasm we agreed to go all the way to Devon next time, expecting him to run well over hurdles on the fast, sunbaked going. The Devon and Exeter (jumping only) meetings take place on the crest of a hill with magnificent views, where the sweet scent of gorse comes drifting in on a pretty stiff breeze. The trip (170 miles from London) was long enough for us to turn it into a brief seaside holiday, so we arranged to stay within easy reach of the racecourse. Frances was offered a lift by Auriol Sinclair, who planned to drive there and back in the day with the stable jockey.

Great Haldon is on the main A38 road and very easy to find, but Auriol unfortunately asked the way just once too often at a crucial roundabout. The stander-on-the-corner said: 'Turn left, you can't miss it.' Whereupon she did exactly that and drove smack into the heart of Exeter, to get inextricably stuck there for over an hour. These little contretemps can overtake anyone. We, on the other hand, arrived early as usual at the racecourse, claimed our owners' badges with pride, ate our cheese sandwich and enjoyed the brilliant, windy sunshine as we strolled to find Islay Mist in the stable. Already the lad was leading him quietly round in his smart blue rug with a yellow 'S', but Mick, the travelling head lad, a small grey-haired man who was normally the most reassuring of people, seemed to be more than a little perturbed.

'They've not arrived. Miss Sinclair isn't here. If they

don't get here by one-thirty I'll find you another jockey – don't worry, there are plenty here.'

We certainly did worry. I had no idea what to do. No jockey – no trainer. Mick shrugged it off: 'Leave it to me, madam,' and Willy was saddled in grim silence.

The minutes wore on, all the horses filed into the paddock and we had reached the highest pitch of agitation when shouts were heard. At last we saw Auriol, Frances and Roger haring through the car park. Roger, who is ultra slim and fit, had the best turn of foot and Arthur shouted: 'Hurry, there's only five minutes left', as he dashed past into the weighing-room. In record time Roger changed into my colours and emerged, his cheeks pink with effort, as the jockeys were told to 'get mounted please'.

Islay Mist charged out of the paddock, bounded to the start in kangaroo style and got off nicely. As the field came past the stands he was very well placed and I began to relax and to enjoy the excitement. Round they went, Islay Mist jumping perfectly. I was within an ace of saying: 'He's going very well', when our horse put his foot in a hole, went down on one knee and that was that. My heart must have missed several beats, but thank goodness the horse was uninjured, and came cantering back with only a slight scrape on his leg, looking delighted with life. It had been a long way to go for nothing and bang went a lot more than sixpence that day!

This was just about the least rewarding of our many expeditions. Willy achieved precisely nothing at great expense and to crown it, managed to bruise his foot slightly at exercise a week later. He could not run again until the very last jumping meeting of the season – Stratford-on-Avon on 2nd June. (Oddly enough, that is when the winter game pauses for two months to let the combatants lick their wounds.) By then Willy was used to race meetings, he surveyed the paddock, head high, in a very relaxed way, looking splendid. Unfortunately the martingale that was so helpful in restraining his mad gallop was left off – so Willy flung up his naughty head and shot away like a rocket, battling against his jockey between hurdles till he was cooked. The net result was another expensive failure, and Islay Mist went home happily to spend his summer holiday with Frances. I had one small consolation, when the list of winning National Hunt owners was published in the *Sporting Life*, I was a statistic.

Willy returned to the fray at Plumpton again at the end of August, and ran second in rather a grand hurdle race (the Tote forecast was very pleasant). Our hopes began to soar, but next time out he achieved nothing in a race at Folkestone; we had to look forward to better things at Worcester ten days after that. However, wait for it, Islay Mist had been too virtuous for too long. One morning after schooling on the racecourse at Plumpton, he got away from his lad and galloped off so fast that no one saw which way he had turned at the main road junction. He galloped on for about four miles and was discovered apparently trying to post a letter. The postman told the police he had found a large, friendly brown horse nibbling the pillar box and wished to return it, as the animal had neither a stamp nor an address on it (or words to that effect).

Willy had jarred his legs slightly on the hard high road, so he rested in luxury for three weeks. That's racing. This is where the owner has to master the art of being patient. However, a new list of engagements arrived to set our hearts beating in anticipation.

This time Willy was entered in a Handicap Hurdle against more experienced opponents at Lingfield. Going there after a gap of more than thirty years reminded me of my fearful clanger as a schoolgirl after one of Peter's best potential 'chasers ran there in a selling race. The horse was so idle at home that nobody knew how good it was, and he wanted to make sure it would not be run off its long, gangling legs. It was a gigantic animal with suspect forelegs, and always wore bandages. It surprised everybody by winning in a canter by ten lengths, with Peter swearing blue murder because he thought it would cost a fortune to buy the horse back (winners of selling races must be sold by auction immediately after the race). As the horse was led round, a man next to me said: 'I'm going to have a go at that.' Without thinking, I turned to him and said: 'He's very dicey in front.' My voice (according to Peter) was clear as a bell and the bidding stopped at £400. Whether this unfortunate remark was really heard I cannot say, but Peter was absolutely furious. It was the only time he ever got angry with me. As it happened, the horse turned out to be a star two-mile 'chaser. Now I whisper comments, unless I particularly want something to be heard. For instance, if our horse has been off colour and may need a race to bring him into serious consideration, I would rather people did not risk their money.

The day we claimed our owners' badges at Lingfield, not one newspaper mentioned our horse. I asked Mick, the travelling head lad, what our chances were. He said: 'What's to beat him?' Valerie, the stable secretary, was just as confident, but I was very doubtful after Folkestone.

Willy bounded to the start more powerfully than ever, martingale and all. I need not have worried. Although another horse set up a commanding lead, ours jumped better than any of them and proceeded to win by six lengths. Making disgraceful hunting noises and Indian war whoops, I ran to greet him in yet another silence. He had been the outsider of the party again at 8 to 1. The forecast payout was delightful and one of my colleagues, Les Carpenter, had the courage to back him with all runners (this is a very good bet if you are confident that an outsider will just about win). Islay Mist had proved himself and we could hardly believe our good fortune. What's more, he had begun to pay for his keep by winning an £800 race.

A major part of the pleasure of being an owner was ringing up my partner to go over every moment of the race as soon as it was established that all was well – no bumps, no bruises, no cuts, had he eaten up? And to speculate about next time.

After the thrills of Lingfield, Islay Mist was entered in the much 'classier' £1,000 Ladbroke Hurdle at Windsor. This was flying high, but we were less diffident nowadays, almost verging on the *blasé*, even recognized by the attendants as we drove into the Owners' car park on 11th November. Again Islay Mist was disregarded by the tipsters and started at 8 to 1. There were fourteen runners, and the odds were not very flattering, but he might have won if the winner had not jumped across him two hurdles from home. We were second in a good finish all the same, and a stranger came up afterwards to ask me why I had not objected. Of course one cannot object when an incident takes place so far from the winning post, unless there has been a very serious interference.

Being second in such a good race was good enough for me. Now Willy was launched at an even bigger prize: the £1,500 Carta Carna Hurdle at Folkestone, over a longer distance, 2½ miles. There was much more confidence in him now; not only was he napped by the *Financial Times* (roll of drums), but tipped by several other papers (martial music). In the unfailingly lovely weather we had learnt to associate with our precious horse, we sat happily munching a cheese sandwich, full of hope.

Willy was in terrific form that day, he collected admiring comments in the paddock because he had reached that peak of fitness when the whole structure of a racehorse seems to be perfectly tuned and rippling with energy. I kissed him on the nose for luck and took a good stare at the opposition.

Going racing with a trainer, I had soon learnt to keep out of the way when he was talking to the owners, the jockey, or anyone else for that matter, which gave me plenty of time to consider the horses in the paddock on my own, and I still enjoy doing precisely that same thing now. I try to notice everything about them, to judge their condition – turn-out – soundness. Ever since, if I cannot see the horses before every race, the race meeting is of no interest (except at Ascot watching from a box, which bears no resemblance to ordinary racing – this is an occasion decorated by superb horses in a superb setting).

The other runners were not very impressive. Willy decided to be as tiresome as possible when the jockey appeared, whirling round madly, then catapulting himself to the start in exaggerated bounces. But we were used to this and thoroughly enjoyed seeing him hit the front half a mile from home, when suddenly, out of the blue, a big, blinkered horse travelling even faster passed Willy, who finished second again.

After this burst of activity there had to be a lull – like any athlete, a horse can get overtrained or tired of the struggle. So can the owner – but that's his lookout.

In *Chaseform* 1971/1972 Islay Mist's record was 00140020122 and he had paid his way. The thrills he had given to Frances, Nigel, Arthur and me were miles beyond our wildest hopes after only two duck's eggs at the very beginning.

Islay Mist went back into training in time to fly very high indeed: the Imperial Cup in 1973 was our objective and this race had pleasant memories for a special reason. When I was sixteen, a second racing dream had shown me a brown horse winning at Sandown, with the jockey in red and green colours. I wrote this down at the time, but those colours did not turn up until about six months later when Peter took me to the Imperial Cup meeting. I was mooching about near the paddock as usual, looking at the horses, considering what to back, when in came a jockey in the self-same red and green colours. I only waited to see him get up on a brown horse before rushing to the Tote – risking two shillings each way. My dream came true at 9 to 1 – what a beauty!

In 1973 the race was moved to Kempton while Sandown Park was being reconstructed. Auriol entered Willy in a high-class handicap hurdle race there in February to see how he measured up against really good horses. After being off the course for two months he obviously needed the race, but our horse had never looked better, he stalked round the paddock as if he was inspecting the crowd. Colin (his lad) won the £25 award, which is given before a number of important races for the best turned out horse.

That day he ran the best race of his life in exalted company; he went with the leaders all the way to finish about fifth. A racing acquaintance came up to me afterwards: 'That horse of yours ran a blinder,' she said. High praise indeed. We were thrilled, but when Imperial Cup day came, Willy chose that occasion to be caught flat-footed at the start with his back to the tape. He might just as well have stayed at home. The huge field went off at a blistering pace and he never caught up with the leaders. We forgave him.

There was always next time to look forward to, and we went back to Lingfield to take on a much less impressive lot of hurdlers in very soft going. Poor Willy was bumped into as he took off at the last hurdle but one, and the hurdle swung back and hit him on the shin. He came in very lame, with a badly bruised foreleg. That's racing.

For the rest of the summer Frances looked after him. He thoroughly enjoyed eating his head off in the sun, but insisted on being brought indoors when the flies were tiresome, or if it was too wet. By now Willy was very spoilt indeed and he made quite a fuss, neighing and stamping at the gate if Frances kept him waiting.

My eye problem had not been conquered, and I now faced the prospect of another minor operation at Moorfields in October, on a date which coincided with Islay Mist's first Autumn engagement at Fontwell Park, near Chichester. I asked for special permission to check in late, thinking that a day's racing would make the best possible prelude. Our horse looked fairly well, but for once he was very quiet in the paddock, and cantered to the start without a single bounce. All the same, we had our share of the excitement, because he ran very well indeed to be second.

I suppose it would have been ideal to lead in the winner on that day, more so because it turned out to be the last time Islay Mist ran a good race. His next appearance at Plumpton puzzled us all – was he tired of racing? Ungenuine perhaps? There was certainly something wrong and after another disappointing run, he managed to be third in a good class hurdle race. Willy always loved his racing. In fact he seemed to revel in it; but now the picture was changed, so we sent him off on holiday. This time Frances could not look after him, because one of those sweet little Welsh pony foals had kicked her on the knee (in the friendliest possible spirit, no doubt), badly breaking her leg. Auriol arranged for Willy to be turned out to grass at stables near Lewes, so that she could keep an eye on him for us. One horrible day the telephone rang and, sounding most unhappy, she said: 'I don't like the look of your Willy, nor does the vet. I know how upset Frances will be, but we must have a second opinion, so I thought you would rather talk it over with her . . .' This was utterly unexpected. But almost at once the news followed, from the expert to whom he had been sent, that dear Willy was incurably ill – he had an internal growth – and we had to say goodbye to him.

Even now, three years later, Frances and I can hardly bear to talk about it. Willy had pranced so happily into our lives, always fighting to win every race, doing his very best. It was a pretty crushing blow, and we miss him dreadfully. I believe that if a little bay filly called Ashdown Forest had not been part of the family by then, this blow would have been the end of a glorious adventure. I still find it hard to recapture the intense excitement dear Willy generated.

6

A Horse of Another Colour

In the late summer of 1972, the news that Islay Mist's brother was for sale started a chain reaction that ended in my suffering from a second attack of ownership. We could not afford to buy him, but the letters, telephone calls and discussions and general excitement about such a tempting possibility may have been responsible. Let us say that Willy's success went to my head. Anyway, more temptation suddenly materialized in a letter from solicitors in Edinburgh telling me that my grandmother had left me £383 5s. 2d., which was my share of an obscure trust fund. As she had died as far back as 1925, this was a long shot of the most surprising kind and obviously destined to be horse money.

So I asked Auriol to find me another horse. She was not exactly wild with enthusiasm when she learnt the size of my windfall, and pointed out that you could not get much for £400. Islay Mist had cost much less, but he was dismissed as the sort of miracle that does not strike in the same place twice. However, Auriol did know of a filly foal by Bivouac, sire of some good hurdlers and 'chasers, which was to be sold at Ascot on the Monday next. Auriol had trained the filly's brother to be placed several times as a two-year-old, before he was sold and went on to win races abroad. She thought the filly would not fetch a high price as she was not fashionably bred, but could be a good investment at my sort of level. Having seen the foal recently, Auriol knew it to be in good order, although rather small. There was no time for me to inspect the animal myself, because it was at Dorothea Hallam's farm in Sussex where Auriol's horses rest between campaigns, or recover from their battle scars. However, after studying the essential pedigree to find the right sort of names on both sides, I decided to have a go with a £400 limit.

Looking back at the whirlwind speed of the transaction that followed, it is hard for me to believe how coolly I decided to bid for an unseen thoroughbred with so little in the kitty, and with not much more thought than I would have given to buying a new hat. This was a long-term, incalculable risk and expensive too, because nearly a year would pass before the filly would be broken in, and anything up to three years before she could appear on the racecourse as a novice hurdler.

Here I was, about to go to Ascot Sales in two days' time, knowing that Frances could not join in my second madness. But I remembered that Les Carpenter, for years a colleague at Country Life Ltd, had once said that he might be interested in sharing a horse with me. In the early days when I was Editor of *Homes and Gardens* he had seen me studying the racing results and I found that he knew very much more about racing than I did. Les rose steadily to the top of the International Publishing Company's tall tree and while he was outpacing his contemporaries, he took a keen interest in Islay Mist. The success of my wild plunge into racing was so infectious that when I asked if he would like to be my partner he said: 'Yes.' We decided to keep the foal on ice, so to speak, as a 'store' in racing parlance, to run over hurdles as a three-year-old at the earliest.

I now looked forward with childish excitement to

attending the sales and as a bidder too, after resisting and resisting the urge to bid for winners of selling races for so many years, even when there was no money in the bank. But it was not to be. The night before the sales, the virus attacked me, so while I fought the 'flu bugs, Auriol and Mrs Hallam escorted the foal to Ascot early in the morning without me. At 10 a.m. the telephone broke into my headache: 'I bought the filly,' said Auriol, 'lucky you didn't come, it's pouring, dreadful day – I had to pay a little bit more than you said, but there's a man near me waiting to take her off your hands if you don't want her.'

'How much?' I croaked.

'Four hundred and eighty pounds.'

'I'll have her,' I said firmly. 'Can Mrs Hallam look after her?' So the foal went home again. The price had been low because few people had arrived by the time she came into the ring – later she would have been way beyond my reach. This is how expensive bargains are come by and believe me they can be very expensive indeed. On hearing that I had bought the foal, Arthur immediately said he would like to take a hand, so the partnership was turned into a threesome.

As soon as possible we went to meet our unknown quantity in a state of wild surmise to say the least. There she stood, in the yard at Dorothea Hallam's farmhouse, more like a very tall, shaggy pony than a racehorse, a sort of animated hearthrug on stilts, with a coat like a grizzly bear, big ears and long whiskers, but quite adorable. A bright bay with a white star on her forehead, big eyes and an impish expression, she stared at us boldly. Although she had been taught to walk along quietly enough, when Dorothea let her loose for us to see her better, she was exceptionally active, bounding round the paddock and rolling till she was plastered with mud. I had not met such a young thoroughbred at close quarters before and found it very difficult to imagine what sort of a horse she would grow to be. It was all most exciting.

On 1st January 1973 the foal officially became a yearling and we had the fun of choosing a name, to register with her 'passport' description. The details of breeding, markings, sex, age, etc. are carefully recorded, because at times over many years, several betting *coups* have been organized by substituting a different, better horse for a poor performer. These 'ringers' are produced every so often, but one only hears of them when they are detected. Edgar Wallace once wrote a novel about a fiddle of this kind, and a major attempt at a *coup* was uncovered within the last two years. It seems an awful lot of trouble to go to, and imagine the problems if, on the day when the great fraud was to take place, the horse was coughing.

Registering a name is not all that easy because so many thousands have been chosen already. Names should not contain more than fifteen letters and must be pure as the driven snow. I have always liked 'Aureulupi' which is best pronounced 'Are you loopy', but gave awful trouble to some commentators who rarely got it right. We wrote down a long list of possible names and after going into a huddle, chose Ashdown Forest, because the dam, Hammerwood, had been called after a village near the forest, so with Bivouac as the sire this seemed appropriate. The name was luckily available. My racing interests had now increased and I was the registered owner of half a hurdler and one-third of a yearling.

The name was quickly shortened to 'Allie' because of a Jack Russell terrier we often saw at race meetings. The little dog was a natural clown. It leapt out of a smart chauffeur-driven car, bouncing and dashing round like a teetotum, then it attacked the nearest yellow 'marker' in the car park, shaking it 'dead' as if it were a rat. Its name was Allie and the naughty look in our foal's eye reminded us irresistibly of the terrier, so the nickname stuck. It was a great pleasure to call to see how Allie was getting on, to watch her develop, first into rather a gawky young lady, who seemed to grow in snatches like any teenager, then suddenly – only a few months later – she blossomed out of her winter fur and began to look like a miniature racehorse.

The months slipped by, then in July, Les and Stella Carpenter and I combined a call on Mrs Hallam to admire Allie with a day's racing at Goodwood. We were all delighted with her progress, and it was thrilling to go there as partners for the first time. By then our filly was in her bright, shining, summer coat, looking very well indeed. However, it was pretty clear that as racehorses go, she was destined to be a little one, so any idea of owning a future steeplechaser became rather remote. Apart from being small, she was definitely naughty and already hated standing still.

It takes ages to train two-year-olds. They have to be broken in as yearlings in the autumn to run the following year. The early birds that pop up and win right at the beginning of the season, disappear almost as quickly – unless they happen to be exceptionally good. When we went to Lewes in February 1973, Ashdown Forest, now aged two, was being ridden out on the downs and we had the fun of seeing both our horses at exercise. Allie looked more grown up, but already her wayward, overactive temperament was noticeable, she was always on the move and even made an ugly face at me when I was too slow getting the Polomints out of their packet. Our little treasure was neither bred nor intended to be an early sort, so it was a nice surprise to hear that she would be forward enough to run as a two-year-old in May or June. It suddenly occurred to me that quite soon I would have a runner on the flat. This was much more than I had hoped for and in a fever of excitement new colours, silks this time, were ordered from Newmarket.

When the partnership saw Ashdown Forest next, she was working on the gallops in the usual stiff breeze and keener than ever. She looked much fitter and my pulse began to race a bit as Auriol's two-year-olds cantered past with Allie among them. No one can predict the actual merit of a horse until it appears on the racecourse where all questions have to be answered. Is he fast? Will he stay five furlongs? Is that not far enough? Perhaps he'll make up into a stayer. Is he a battler? Will those joints stand up to it? Most two-year-olds race over five furlongs first, later they tackle six furlongs and, eventually, a mile. By the time they have run two or three times, it is usually clear which will be the most suitable distance. Ashdown Forest's first appearance was to be at Brighton at the end of May and we made sure that Frances would come over to meet the new partnership and help us celebrate having a runner on the flat for a change.

Tremendous interest was aroused when Auriol raised the question of a jockey for this all-important first appearance. She did not have a flat race jockey attached to her stable at the time, but suggested Bobby (R. P.) Elliott, who is a fine horseman and we were very pleased when he accepted the ride.

Knowing that Allie could be rather wayward, I was frankly apprehensive. I had watched so many two-year-olds being led into the paddock, eyes staring, head high, wearing a neat little rug (not the one that got chewed up last week, but a smart one for the paddock) with a large black number on a white background. They mince round, regarding the spectators with amazement and, if very inexperienced, occasionally stop to neigh in desperate tones, or dart about on the end of the leading rein like a hooked fish, dragging the lad/lass across the grass. Sometimes this ends in a loose horse (not mine for goodness sake!) dashing about aimlessly, bashing against the railings and returning, slightly dented, to try again another day. However, the parade is soon over and the jockeys are asked to get mounted please by a sepulchral voice on the intercom (this can cause another stampede with very babyish two-year-olds). All the ones which had been behaving like angels now decide that the jockeys are terrifying and it's time to go home. Round and round in circles they go, but with help from trainer, lad, and travelling head lad in concerted action, the jockeys get aboard, wisely keeping their feet clear of the stirrups until the horses decide to co-operate. Next move – leave the paddock, quietly if possible.

I went to see Ashdown Forest being dressed up in a sheepskin 'muff' nose-band, to stop her running with her head in the air, an elastic breastgirth to prevent the saddle slipping and a leather neckstrap to give the jockey a finger grip when/if she played up. She emerged, alert and ready for action, then surprised us all by behaving perfectly in the paddock, not even blinking at my shiny new silks, so much brighter than the familiar jersey variety and even easier to see. Les Carpenter had not arrived, so the little group that admired my first runner in a flat race was the original 'old firm' – Frances, Nigel, Arthur and me. Our filly looked rather small and not so forward in condition as the others, but nothing mattered. It was such a thrill to be there, at Brighton on a lovely sunny day with Allie safely on the way to the starting gate, that I could hardly believe it.

Les and Stella Carpenter got there only just in time to watch her canter down, or rather up, the steep hill to the stalls, and it was here that she decided to make her presence felt. Through binoculars we could see every runner walk quietly into the stalls, except Allie who kept alternately backing away, or standing on end. She was tired of waiting, but at last they shoved her in, and she was off. Once out of the gate and away on the flat, the only obstacles are the other horses. Your horse can be kicked, banged into the rails, crossed, bumped or brought down, that is if it doesn't slip up on a bend, cross its legs, jump a path, or shy at the crowd. Ashdown Forest came zipping happily round the bend at the top of the hill, then swerved violently. She had been hacked on the shin – that's racing. The net result of her thrilling first appearance was a long, long holiday, which was spent eating Dorothea's lovely green grass until the virus took its toll. My silks stayed in just about mint condition, because our filly could not run again until the autumn.

At long last Ashdown Forest was declared to run over five furlongs again, but at Lingfield, with another jockey, a very successful apprentice called T. Cain, who could claim 7 lbs. She behaved admirably and ran well enough for him to say that he would like the chance to ride her as a three-year-old next season. We now settled down to the owner's traditional pastime of waiting and waiting and waiting, while Allie spent the winter at Mrs Hallam's farm. In *Racehorses of 1974* she is described as: '6th of 9 in maiden race in November. Should be suited by 1m+.' In recent years this book, a comprehensive study of form, has become the bible of the racing world. It lists every horse in training with its record from the first time out, till the end of each season, giving it a rating which starts with the best horse of the year at say 148, descending to 0 and awarding additional 'black marks' in the shape of sinister squiggles which can label the horse:

One squiggle: somewhat ungenerous, faint hearted or a bit of a coward – unreliable;

Two squiggles: an arrant rogue, or thorough jade.

At least one unfortunate animal has been awarded four squiggles – need I say more? In 1976 a similar book was produced for jumping and in the jumping world X is the bad mark, it means: not a good jumper. Two X's mean a very poor jumper. I think the saddest rating is d – for deteriorated. This book gives me hours of happy study and I hope my husband will remember it as a star birthday present. Every spring I leave the old book lying about prominently just in case. Some of the definitions repay a little study, and I wonder which would be the least acceptable if one was a horse. They descend from: 'probably of little account' through 'seemingly of little account' (a very fine shade of opinion here) to 'of little account', in a sad declension, to 'poor maiden', so forlorn, to 'poor plater', to 'very poor plater' down to the absolute 'of no account', but there is even worse to come in the final verdict: 'useless'. However affectionate, beautiful, well meaning, well bred and co-operative your horse may be, on the racecourse it is labelled useless. But do not despair, there are plenty of exceptions to revive a quailing owner. Many a racehorse in the 'of no account' list on the flat has won over hurdles and in 1977, already at least one horse labelled (or libelled perhaps?) 'of little account' won three times in four attempts, which is good enough for most people.

Years ago, a beautifully bred yearling fetched a record price at the sales and thousands of pounds changed hands. The horse was called Tuppence, which represented his true value, because he only won one little race. This is all part of the game. It would certainly be interesting to find out what our filly was worth.

As a three-year-old, Ashdown Forest could be entered in maiden races until, after running three times, she would be given a handicap rating. Auriol chose Windsor as a suitable venue, because it is accessible for Londoners like ourselves and an easy course, although with its figure-of-eight layout, there are bends to negotiate. The choice is very wide, and it is for the trainer to decide which distance, and which course is most suitable, and to suggest a jockey (unless there is a jockey attached to the stable, as there is at every big establishment, with an apprentice as well). Auriol still had no stable jockey for flat racing, but there are plenty to choose from, and for Allie's reappearance at Windsor over a mile and a quarter we all agreed that an apprentice (claiming 7 lbs) would be ideal and were glad to hear that T. Cain, who had ridden her at Lingfield, was available again.

We drove to Windsor for an evening meeting at the end of May, delighted at the prospect of seeing our filly on the racecourse again; and arrived in the usual state of excitement which does not seem to wear off — however many times, however many disappointments, it is always just as thrilling — to find that Allie had filled out; she looked very strong and very pleased with herself. Then, as the horses were led into the paddock, our little darling decided to erupt. She stood on end, bucked, charged first one way, then the other, doing her best to cause the maximum trouble while the other horses walked round, good as gold. It was very shaming. At last the jockeys appeared, which was her cue to put on a rodeo performance. It took the jockey all his time to get into the saddle, Allie stood up on end, tried to buck him off, then charged out of the paddock, cannoning into both sides of the exit and dashed to the right, while the goodies went dutifully to the left. The jockey did very well to stay on and to pull up, finally managing to turn Allie facing the right way, at which she chose to proceed past the stands in a series of fly jumps like a ballet dancer on stilts, to the delight of the spectators (except us).

I was a nervous wreck by the time, ages after the runners were being put into the stalls, Ashdown Forest joined them. Would she go in? My heart was pounding away. Like an old hand, Allie walked into the stalls, only to shoot out again like a scalded cat, hurtling to the front, where she stayed for nearly a mile. The commentator mentioned no other horse as she scuttled along ahead of a big field, till she reached the bend before the finishing straight, then as they came into the last quarter of a mile, she dropped back. She had run out of steam. At least my colours had blazed the trail and Allie seemed all set for a fine career if she would just calm down a bit. We were very encouraged in spite of such a hectic start and looked forward to 'better things next time'.

Ashdown Forest seemed as full of bounce after the race as before, and we wondered if a shorter distance, a mile instead of a mile and a quarter, might be better? After much telephoning to consult Auriol, who was ill and had not been at Windsor, we heard that there were several suitable races in the offing. But now, believe it or not, a totally new (to me) factor created another delay. Allie had grown 'wolf teeth', rather like human wisdom teeth which had to be extracted and which might have caused her to be so difficult to ride. However, she was finally declared to run in a mile maiden race at Newbury in mid-July. It was very pleasant to arrive at one of our favourite racecourses as an owner on a lovely summer's day. Ashdown Forest was unfortunately not at her best and made such a scene at the start that she was put into the stalls first, where she waited, fussing and fuming till the other runners were ready. She got off poorly and found herself like the meat in the sandwich, small and jostled by the bigger horses, and ran a very poor race indeed.

We looked at each other in dismay. Whatever next? It was so totally unexpected to see her outpaced and dreary. It felt like a slap in the face with a wet fish after that promising début at Windsor. The more we talked about it the less clear the picture became. Eventually,

Auriol asked us to let Allie run over a much shorter distance, six furlongs only, as an experiment – and we converged rather reluctantly on Folkestone 'just to see'. This was another disappointment about which words would be a waste. So we decided unanimously to turn Allie out to grass to mature, to grow and, hopefully, to grow up until she could run over hurdles. My bright silks certainly had very little wear during those two blankly abortive flat-racing seasons. This meant reverting to the original plan – Ashdown Forest was bred to be a hurdler, but certainly still seemed definitely too small for a potential steeplechaser, which was very tiresome.

By then Frances and Nigel had moved to Nantgaredig in South Wales to a farm with plenty of grazing, and that is where Ashdown Forest was sent for six months. Frances had always promised to look after her, now that Islay Mist was gone, so she introduced our wayward and expensive investment to the delicious green grass of Wales.

There is no doubt that Allie has a very naughty streak – just occasionally, she got above herself and tried to push Frances out of the box. Often she would stand gazing out over the valley, refusing to go indoors, or walk round the field in circles, instead of coming to be caught, just to annoy. Once my sister left Allie out all night to teach her a lesson. There was no nonsense next time. Although Frances found her maddening at times, she became very fond of her because Allie loved to be fussed over and to have her ears stroked, although if her food did not turn up on time, she made very cross faces and it was unwise to get between her and the manger.

After a great deal of thought, advice from Auriol and discussions with Les, we decided to find a trainer near the Welsh borders, because the Carpenters go racing at Chepstow from Evesham at week-ends, and it seemed logical to base the filly nearer to their part of the world. I wrote to John Edwards, who runs a most successful stable near Leominster, and asked if he would inspect Ashdown Forest with a view to taking her into training as a hurdler. He went over to my sister's farm quite soon and then telephoned to say that he liked the look of our filly, although she was rather small, and in May 1976 she joined his string and a new era of anticipation began.

Arthur and I between us now owned another hurdler called Makadir (see next chapter) and we began to wonder how to fit in both their engagements when the jumping season began. It seemed a very short time before a postcard came from John Edwards announcing Ashdown Forest's first appearance as a four-year-old in a $1\frac{1}{2}$ mile flat race at Haydock on 6th August 1976. Our wild-goose chases had already taken us far and wide. Islay Mist ran at Wye, Plumpton, Lingfield, Folkestone, Devon and Exeter, Kempton, Windsor, Stratford-on-Avon and Fontwell. Allie had taken us to Newbury, and on the long trek to Haydock, which was very kindly shortened by my partner inviting us to stay the night en route. Les was away so Stella drove us there.

It was a lovely day which went with a swing from the moment when a total stranger hailed me in the car park saying how much he had enjoyed meeting me in Hong Kong. We had a crazy surrealistic conversation, because I have never been farther east than Constantinople, but it was all very friendly and he was left with his illusions.

Haydock is a delightful racecourse with tall trees shading the paddock. Although this was our first visit as owners, we had enjoyed a racing holiday there once before, but going there 'on business' so to speak, is a totally different matter. The worry and the thrills combine to turn an outing into a wild adventure. Mrs Edwards and I went off to find Allie who was in splendid condition, nicely muscled up, her bright bay coat gleaming with health.

It was lovely to see her again, she looked totally different from the shaggy individual I had visited in Wales. Knowing the form on previous occasions, I warned the lad that Allie was apt to play up in the paddock but she walked in on her very best behaviour and I was grateful to hear a spectator say: 'That one's got a lot of quality about it.' No sooner had Allie reached the paddock entrance again, than she whipped round, doing her best to drag the lad back to the stables. However, this 'demo' was nothing like as bad as I feared and she went to the start chaperoned by both Mrs Edwards and the lad, giving no trouble whatever. Dennis McKay, the jockey who rode her, is very strong indeed and kept such a tight hold on the reins that she had no opportunity to do more than walk crab-wise to the stalls. As the gate opened she went off like a rocket, head in the air in spite of a nose band, fighting all the way, and after being in the first three coming into the straight, as before, she blew up. This was thought to be quite a satisfactory effort after such a very long interval, but John Edwards said she needed more weight on her back, and a jockey with longer legs. So he entered her in an Amateur Flat race at Kempton where she was allotted 11 stone 8 lbs, top weight in a big field.

Allie had never raced under such a heavy burden before and, not surprisingly, settled down much better. Oddly enough she was giving weight to all the other runners, although she is so small, but she managed to be fifth of fourteen and the horse that was fourth carried $1\frac{1}{2}$ stone less. If only she would 'settle' instead of insisting on making the running, this could be most encouraging. Her next race was planned to be over hurdles at level weights, against other four-year-old novices.

The ground in the autumn of 1976 was as hard as a brick after the drought, so Allie could not be schooled over hurdles safely, but John Edwards jumped her over straw bales instead and at last a postcard came:

		Ashdown Forest		
Date	*Meeting*	*Race*	*Value*	*Distance*
Aug 30th	Southwell	Tuxford Novice Hurdle	£400	2m

This was indeed a modest target – but one has to start somewhere and anything can happen the first time out. Some novice hurdlers have a way of bolting for about half a mile, shattering the hurdles as they come to them, then blowing up and returning at a slow walk (pulled up). The alternative is to dash at the first hurdle, stop dead staring in amazement at the obstacle, then take a standing leap over it, leaving the jockey half-way between Oh Lord and Thank God, as the next hurdle looms ahead. Allie did much better than that. She jumped pretty well and was third at the first attempt, with Les and Stella to cheer her on. I could not get away and for the very first time my colours appeared without me. She had earned us £33 in three years.

For a while Ashdown Forest seemed fated to explore the far reaches of the Welsh borders on impossible dates. Her list of engagements included Bangor-on-Dee, Hereford and Uttoxeter – and next time was awaited with more excitement than ever because we knew that Allie could jump. Les and Stella went off hopefully to Bangor-on-Dee (again I could not get there) where she started co-favourite and led all the way. But after the last hurdle she just about stopped and only finished fourth. She pulled up with a bruised foreleg, after which she retired to her box for yet another rest. That's racing. There would be no problem about running two horses!

. . . . .

I hate to admit failure, but owning Ashdown Forest has been a nightmare of frustration, ever since that first run when she was kicked on the shin and then caught the virus. By the time she was five years old she had managed to be third then fourth in exceptionally poor hurdle races. However, I suppose my place among the racing fraternity was acknowledged for the first time when a very grand lady who knew me well, but rarely bothered to smile if I caught her eye, came up to me at Newbury and asked: 'How's the hawss?' It was rather fun to answer 'Which one?' She looked quite baffled as I walked on, studying my race card. And soon after Ashdown Forest's second appearance in a hurdle race, I was walking towards the paddock at Kempton when a friend winked at me and asked: 'And how's your extensive string?' The mathematics of one-half, plus one-third are rather too difficult for me, but when Arthur was no longer well enough to go winter racing, he gave up his 'interest' in the horses, so Les Carpenter and I shared Allie equally.

1977 had turned from the wettest of known winters into the wettest of known springs by the time Allie was fit enough to return to work. She had not changed her style of racing and went off as usual, blew up as usual, but was given another chance. In fact one engagement would have been at Southwell near Newark at a fantastic meeting which drew 187 horses into its web, but the weather clamped down so that only seven out of the thirteen races were run. Imagine thirteen races in one day — that is only surpassed by the all-time record at Hereford when fourteen races actually took place. The going must have been beyond description by the end of the afternoon. Allie's second run was no more encouraging, sadly enough, so after much thought we decided to run her in a selling race on the flat over a mile and a quarter to see how she got on, as two miles over hurdles appeared to be just too far.

Windsor was the venue again and one perfectly beastly cold, dripping wet evening in May 1977 we stood with the raindrops falling on our heads and everywhere else too, while Allie, looking exceptionally well and behaving impeccably, sauntered round the paddock. She did not seem so small and was certainly very pleased with herself, so I made a beeline for the Tote and risked £2 for a win and £3 for a place on her. Dennis McKay rode her again in a field of fourteen. Allie, however, was not going to let us get away without nervous tension – she was the very last to leave the paddock and most reluctant about it, but came quietly crab-wise past the stands, till suddenly she shied and sent the jockey flying over her head. He kept hold of the reins, thank goodness, and with a sigh of relief we saw him hop on again. History repeated itself – Allie walked into the stalls last, shot out like a scalded cat and led all the way for over a mile, then first one horse passed her, then another, but this time she fought back and battled on to be second at 20 to 1. We were absolutely delighted – how any owner can be so pleased at seeing a five-year-old mare run second in a selling race, I cannot possibly explain, but it had been a very long wait with so little hope of success. We had won £109. It felt marvellous and the Tote paid 7 to 1 for a place – what a beauty.

7

While the Grass Grows

True to form, instant decision-making had once again been the keynote back in Autumn 1974 when a third racehorse arrived to hit me in the cheque book. This came about because Arthur noticed how sadly I missed meeting Frances, Nigel and Willy on the racecourse; all the planning, the celebrations, even the disappointments, which added up to such a compelling interest. Ashdown Forest up till now had not been an adequate substitute, so he decided to find me a consolation prize. At the same time, my eye problem proved to be insoluble, so a cheering-up expedition to Lewes to see how Allie was getting on seemed to be a nice idea. We set off to lunch with Auriol, driving through the narrow, deep green lanes towards the downs, and as we passed the familiar signpost to Plumpton, Arthur suddenly said: 'Would you like another hurdler?' There are no prizes for guessing my answer. I could hardly believe it. Evidently Arthur had seen one of Auriol's young hurdlers called Makadir win a novice race at Kempton and liked his looks. Now the horse was for sale so we were going to consider buying him on the hoof, ready-made, fit and due to run again having won a sponsored hurdle race first time out after his summer holiday.

I watched Makadir canter up for us to inspect him in a

dream, the day seemed quite unreal – to think we were considering buying a potential steeplechaser, already a proved success, only six years old. The horse had run four times in all – winning twice and being placed second once, which was impressive enough. Quite a contrast between my other ventures, an unbroken two-year-old and a small filly foal, and this good-looking, fit, keen gelding by Kadir Cup out of a winner of many point-to-points, Martha Gunn.

By lunch-time a third money-eating equine liability had landed on my bank balance, but Arthur luckily promised to share the training bills. We had bought Makadir with his engagements to discover that it would not be long to wait, because he was entered in an Opportunity Hurdle (for apprentice riders only) at Ascot in a week's time (the transfer of ownership does not take long). Such a grand venue added even more excitement to Makadir's first appearance, wearing the smart blue and white brow band Frances had given me for Allie's bridle. Colin Bowen, the lad who had always 'done' Islay Mist, was then apprenticed to Auriol's stable so he rode Makadir.

For the winter game, the paddock at Ascot is arranged just below the grandstand and we walked in, full of hope because our horse was 'expected'. He started at 9 to 2, second favourite in a field of twenty. Makadir looked magnificent in the paddock, his black coat gleaming; he certainly stood out and must have decided to enjoy his day to the full. He bounced away from the start, took more or less complete charge and dashing to the front, gave away his chances, only managing to finish sixth. Oh dear.

Now began a series of utterly maddening, but nearly always exciting experiences. Mak had run well enough for us to look forward, with incurable optimism, to the next race, this time with his usual jockey Roger Rowell, riding. However, believe it or not, our horse could not run again till Christmas, because he was coughing. That's racing. When he eventually arrived to run at Kempton, it was so wet that there were puddles of water in the grass, even in the paddock, and the soft going certainly appeared not to suit him at all. The next, and in 1975 just about inevitable, event was the virus – which kept our horse on the sick list till the early autumn, when at long last he ran well enough on firm going at Sandown to start us hoping again.

In the book *Chasers and Hurdlers of 1975-76*, Makadir is described as: 'Rangy gelding, fair hurdler, stays $2\frac{1}{2}$ miles, acts on heavy going.' Those last four words unfortunately remain a mystery. He certainly hasn't acted well on heavy going yet.

I soon found myself in the train on the way to Nottingham with Auriol (Arthur was ill) to see Mak run in a good class handicap on a fine March day, full of hope. When we got there, ice was forming in the puddles and the jockeys said there were slippery patches. Mak took full advantage of a strange jockey (Roger Rowell had injured his wrist), stuck his naughty head in the air, slithered on every bend and was generally very tiresome, to no avail. Auriol and I discussed his future all the way home in the train and decided to send him steeplechasing. First he would go to be schooled by Eric Thompson, the three-day event expert, who would stop him dashing off and spoiling his chances every time.

I had always wanted to send Mak 'chasing, and looked forward greatly to this new venture, which is by far the most spectacular kind of race. As they slow up (like you and me in middle age) a great many hurdlers who are still sound in wind and limb turn into budding steeplechasers.

Will they jump the big fences? Well, sometimes. Novice steeplechases are the most hair-raising equestrian events ever devised to test the nerves; there is something particularly gladiatorial about them. The antics some normal, apparently sane horses get up to on facing a plain fence for the first time, let alone an open ditch, are quite frightening. In fact half the horses appear reluctant and the other half incapable. Anyone new to racing might well imagine that many novice 'chasers have not been schooled at all. Some slow down, legs spread awkwardly, noses near the floor, trying not to jump, with the jockeys doing their utmost; others flounder over like crippled donkeys, or, ears pricked, charge at the first fence as if it didn't exist, with fatal results. Others refuse point blank, scuttle along the fence like rabbits, or flop over, sending the unhappy jockey flying (unseated rider).

Jumping big fences makes far more demands on horse and rider than hurdling – the pace is far slower, but the risks are far greater. Fallers over the sticks that get up again and follow round can cause havoc among the runners as they blaze an erratic trail, taking fences at any angle that happens to suit, bringing other horses down or hampering them seriously. There seems to be no answer to this, it is yet another hazard to add to many reasons/excuses for losing a race and makes me wonder once again how anybody ever wins anything. It's rather like playing Snakes and Ladders:

> Slow at start – miss one turn
>
> Go on to fence three
>
> Refuse to jump – go back to square one
>
> Slip up on landing – miss one turn
>
> Go on to fence seven
>
> Hampered by loose horse
>
> Go back to fence four
>
> Hit top of fence nine – disaster!

While this is going on, the other players are probably in trouble too, but as always, someone struggles past the post first.

It is hard to explain why one goes on hoping – but there is something so irresistibly exciting about being at a race meeting once you are directly involved, that all other considerations, logical or financial, do not affect the issue. It is such fun. I still don't know what pleasure there is in writing a huge cheque month after month to keep a lovely looking black elephant in luxury. I cannot even enjoy the other races, when my horse is running. The tension is terrific, partly because the jockey risks a fall and serious injury every time, as does the horse.

Makadir also has an unfortunate weakness, he is a rainmaker – whenever and wherever he is tuned up and ready to run, the heavens open and it rains cats, dogs and Shetland ponies – with thunder in the offing at times, which is frustrating because our horse is at his best on good to firm going. All one season when the going was firm as firm can be, Makadir was recovering in delightful surroundings with a friend, after cutting himself (a deep over-reach on the fetlock) while schooling over the big fences. That's racing. It took months to heal and no sooner was he due to run over hurdles at Towcester, as a reintroduction to the racecourse after such a long gap (Autumn 1976) than the weather changed. It rained and it rained and it rained. We drove over from Helen's house near Market Harborough on a dry but stormy-looking day, watching the dark, threatening cloudscape looming nearer. Then, as we reached Towcester (another racecourse to add to our collection), the rain came down in sheets. Makadir plodded round, obviously disliking every inch of the two and a half miles, leaping over the hurdles as if they were six feet high.

However, we tried to rise above this weird performance

and looked forward to his début in a Novice Steeplechase at Huntingdon (collecting yet another new racecourse) – hopefully on better going. The weather was fine until our turn came. Then the rain came pouring down. Makadir's first effort over the big fences was far from encouraging and my enthusiasm was well and truly damped – like my feet. His efforts at this new game never put his rider at risk, because he is exceptionally careful and, when first confronted by an open ditch, looked pained and grieved, but willing to try.

Although my riding stopped more than thirty-five years ago after a bad fall, even now watching a steeplechase, I cannot help living every second of every jump. When it's my own precious horse I can almost feel him pounding along. I take off and land with him – rally him as he falters and when he pulls up safely, dash off to see that all's well. Patting a dripping wet horse that is blowing hard and waving its head up and down is a doubtful pleasure – but it's all part of racing.

However, dogged does it, and off we went two weeks later to Folkestone, where the going was described as good in the *Sporting Life*, thinking third time lucky, etc. As we got nearer to our target, more and more, bigger and bigger puddles on the edge of the road sparkled ominously. The rain was just ahead. Over Folkestone racecourse – one might have guessed – a cloudburst at 11 a.m. had changed the going completely. Makadir did a little better; however, he again slithered about on the turns and achieved absolutely nothing. So we drove sadly back to London.

This was the point of no return – or jolly nearly. I decided to give him one chance, just one more chance only, to show that he could jump in good company as soon as the going improved. After quite an interval we headed for Kempton, and for once the sun came out. The going was excellent and Makadir suddenly got the message (Jimmy McNaught rode him in spurs), jumped very well if a little carefully, and when the second favourite fell at the last fence, Makadir ran on to be fourth in a big field, over two and a half miles. The Kempton fences are really stiff, so this was very cheering.

Two weeks later, we returned to Huntingdon, but this time (are you surprised?) it rained all the way through Hampstead onto the Great North Road, where it simply pelted when it wasn't pouring. Auriol, Jimmy McNaught and I were equally amazed to find that racing was still possible. Huntingdon is a charming little racecourse, delightfully arranged, but that day it was absolutely sopping — mud everywhere and Makadir a hot favourite at 2 to 1 in a field of 12 was a most unattractive bet. I longed to hang a placard round his shiny neck with 'I hate the mud' on it, but had to watch him walk round the paddock, hidden by a macintosh hood, macintosh sheet, and leggings on all four legs. Only his black nose and his long black tail could be seen and still the rain came down.

Makadir set off in great style, jumping perfectly the first time round, causing an expert on the rails to risk another £20 on him in the running, but on the far side of the course he hit a sticky patch and faltered, dropping back dramatically. Injured? Broken down? Over-reached again? Unenthusiastic? All these possibilities raced through my mind, but from the back of the field he began to run on again. 'Come on, Mak,' I shouted, and with a big effort he managed to be third.

My excitement was such that I forgot to follow Makadir into the unsaddling enclosure. It had been more than two years since Islay Mist stepped into third place for the last time and it was nice to be back, even if stroking a hot, steaming horse on a cold, dripping wet day may seem rather an odd way to spend one's time. There is hardly anything nicer than getting into the frame —

except of course leading in the winner. Makadir had earned £59.90.

Auriol now felt that he would be more effective over a longer distance, so he was entered in a three-mile steeplechase at Newbury in March 1977. The weather was perfect, but the going soft and sticky and there were twelve runners. Our horse 'Chased leader all the way – mistake at second last – no chance'. But it was thrilling to see him jump perfectly, up till that crucial moment, having been in the first three all the way over three miles of stiff fences. The jockey, Jimmy McNaught, was not unseated, and his acrobatic feat in staying on board was quite spectacular. This was a landmark, Makadir had done extremely well but Jimmy McNaught, for whom he went so well, was very badly injured soon afterwards, so another jockey had to be engaged for the next outing which was at Fontwell. Mak again seized the opportunity to do the absolute minimum. He lolloped round, taking every care not to scratch his elegant legs and returned to be unsaddled almost laughing at us, hardly even warm. He had become much too clever.

We decided to put him back to hurdling, over three miles, because he was obviously not going to bother to win a steeplechase. Mak was too cute by far. Some horses, from one day to the next, give up the battle and settle for a quiet life. A really crafty veteran can be a problem. He knows exactly where it is warm and comfortable, so he will often swerve sharply towards the paddock in an attempt to get home early. I saw a horse at Fontwell set off with the others for a two-mile race, but after fifty yards turn smartly to the right and carry his furious jockey straight back the way they had come. I never saw a more smug expression on any animal as he watched his rivals fighting out the finish from a safe distance.

I can only add that the last time Makadir ran had to be in a downpour, and miles away. We left London on a fine, sunny morning, but twenty miles from Warwick the rain started and it simply pelted, with a little sleet here and there for added piquancy. For the first time, after owning three horses, I saw my colours trailing along behind all the way round. The horse obviously would not try any more. That was that. Darling Mak is now on holiday, as pleased with himself as ever. He gave some good exhibitions of jumping at times during those two years and always looked very fine in the paddock — but what did I learn from these experiences?

8

If Wishes were Racehorses

One thing soon began to stick out a mile – you do not own a racehorse, the boot is on the other hoof – the horse owns you. Not only that, it dictates your every single plan, your holidays, your whereabouts and if at any point it should strike you as nice to have a day's racing at Sandown, never fear – the horse will be entered at Wincanton; and if by any chance you happen to want to be on holiday in the west country, the ideal race for your horse is sure to be at Thirsk.

When two horses come into one family simultaneously, worse soon follows. My two stars once seemed fated to twinkle (very faintly indeed in both cases) on the same day, one at Ludlow, Shropshire; the other at Newbury, Berkshire. Nothing could have been less convenient.

The owner has to plod on doggedly, aware that in the complicated pecking order of the racing set-up he comes quite low, particularly at Newbury, where arriving as an owner I expected to drive into the Members' Car Park – oh no – the owners must stay outside like the jockeys and the trainers. One day these will all strike and what will the members do without them? Perhaps they'll organize a five-furlong sprint among themselves?

The order of precedence could be:

1 The breeder
2 The horse
3 The owner
4 The trainer
5 The jockey
6 The spectators, and
7 The bookmaker, who holds the key to the whole complicated puzzle, because it is betting that keeps the racehorse on its expensive feet.

Rather a sobering thought, but there is no other way to explain the presence of thousands of highly fed, decorative, but absolutely useless quadrupeds, who contribute nothing to science, the welfare of nations, or progress. They are the most expensive playthings ever invented, apart from Madame de Pompadour and her counterparts.

When you consider how many people are involved in getting a horse to the starting gate, you face a small army. The trainer, who organizes its career, the lad who actually feeds and grooms the creature, the head lad who watches over its general welfare, the travelling head lad who accompanies it to race meetings, the man who drives the horse-box, the blacksmith, the vet, the fodder merchant, the chap who delivers the wood shavings for the loose-box, the saddler, the Clerk of the Course, the security man at the racecourse stables, the jockey, the jockey's valet, the Clerk of the Scales, the racecourse maintenance staff, the starter, the starter's assistant, the judge — to name only a token handful of officials. Then behind all this is Weatherbys, where the paperwork computes its weary way, with, hovering above the whole of racing, the great deep purple umbrellas of the Jockey Club and the Betting Levy Board. What an intricate set-up, into which colossal spider's web every owner is absorbed. Within it the rules are absolute but do not confine the owner as rigidly as the trainer, or the jockey. The trainer must not give the horse a little something to speed it up, while the jockey must not wilfully slow a horse down (beyond its inclinations) and if either of these characters strays from the straight and narrow, which has been known to happen – that's racing – the owner does not pay the fine. He just loses his shirt and pants when the horse wins, but is disqualified for leaning on the opposition (bumping and boring), tacking wildly across the course, carrying too little weight, or if the jockey fails to weigh in.

The stewards spend hours every year deciding who bumped who and having made that difficult decision, more often than not announce that the result stands. Nowadays television and a head-on camera both provide far better evidence than the human eye ever could, and the car-mounted TV cameras sometimes follow so closely that it takes real artistry to engineer a poor performance. Stewards time and time again send for trainers to ask: 'How come? Two weeks ago it was last of ten, today your horse starts favourite and wins – what a remarkable improvement.' The explanations are usually highly credible: 'Change of going – horse travelled badly – was found to have a temperature – was run off its feet – came back slightly lame.' It's when the explanations sound more like excuses that the situation hardens and a new element creeps in. The explanation is recorded, but if things get too near the knuckle for comfort, a report is forwarded to the Stewards of the Jockey Club, whose authority is supreme.

Imagine the blushes all round, when an earnest, anxious to learn young lady on meeting the Senior Steward of the

Jockey Club, was heard to say: 'I suppose you are in charge of all the catering?'

The owner, however, is really the cornerstone, because he provides the essential horse. It is difficult to decide whether owning a racehorse is a hobby, a craze, a sign of impending lunacy, or just a wild speculation. With all the eggs in one four-legged, headstrong, vulnerable, equine basket (or bits of one), or even in several different ones, a big slice of luck is essential if you hope to break even financially. Showing a profit has been known to be possible, but every owner needs a fairly elastic pocket because the hidden costs are so many and so various that there is no way to estimate them.

I am often asked how much it costs to keep a horse in training and the answer at the time of writing this (but bound to go up even more), is roughly £3,000 a year, and take it from me that whatever figure you first thought of must be doubled. Basic training fees vary from £30 to £50 a week, depending on individual trainers and the locality, plus a fee for gallops which varies tremendously, plus VAT on practically everything. (If you arrange to pay bills via Weatherbys, they make a charge for settling accounts.) Now start to add:

> Shoeing at £10 a time, and when those four precious feet go racing, they have to be unshod to be reshod with special light-weight 'plates' which have to be removed afterwards to replace the first lot. So it certainly mounts up, doesn't it?

Now add on every year:

> Registration of authority for trainer to act – £6.48
>
> Registration of partnership – £1.08
>
> Registration of colours – £4.32

Insurance — 8% for flat racing and hurdling; 10% for 'chasing;

Blood testing — adds to the Veterinary Surgeon's quite heavy charges

Veterinary supplies — imponderable, could be very little until the horse starts the usual run of minor ailments — or an awful shock

Transport — every time a horse goes anywhere (apart from on its own fragile legs) it seems to cost £20. If it goes any distance it's more like £80 — but the Betting Levy Board provides travel allowances for distances over 50 miles from the stables

If you run — the jockeys cost £20 for jumping and £15 for flat racing

Entries — from about £12 a run to absolutely anything!

The list of minor unexpected costs is endless. Then you could add petrol, hotel bills and presents to the lads, but don't start counting your losing bets — you have worries enough already.

Since I started my ownership in 1970, the cost of almost every item has doubled, so of course has the price of both petrol and railway tickets, so if you live in London (as I do) and the horse insists on running at Devon and Exeter, or at Perth if you live in East Kent, it's quite a consideration. However carefully plans are made to avoid unnecessary travel by keeping the entries within a reasonable radius, wait for it — the weather will be the arbiter.

Apart from the actual cost of keeping your racehorse in his gold-plated oats, another major factor is the state of the going. There is no future in racing near London when the ground is like reinforced concrete — if conditions are perfect, say, at Haydock Park. In my experience, whenever you happen *not* to want to race it is always good going. And once that subject comes up, it's quite a study. The going is most often described in terms ranging from hard through to heavy like this:

> Hard; firm; good to firm; good; good to soft; heavy, with yielding or dead thrown in occasionally to complete the picture. That is the usual 'scale' referred to on a notice board in the paddock and in the press, but who can say just how good/firm/soft those three central conditions may be.

Sometimes one expert wisely pronounces: 'It's on the firm side of good', while the next says: 'It's on the good side of firm', or 'it's softer than good' or 'it's not really as soft as all that', *ad infinitum*.

If the experts admit that the going is either hard or very heavy, it probably is, and no horse living can run equally well under those two conditions. There are horses that come sploshing and squelching through the mud, revelling in it; there are top of the ground specialists who like to hear their hooves rattle; but every racehorse appreciates really good going – that is where the excuses have to stop (unless your horse has a leg problem which makes the mud a necessity). The going is a popular tailor-made excuse/reason for failure, because the weather is so utterly unpredictable that conditions can change at any hour, within the hour, and horses cannot! Jockeys are freely quoted as finding the going: 'treacherous – diabolical – slippy on the turns – rock hard – unfit for racing', but just once in a while everyone admits that the going is perfect. Your horse, however, is far from perfect, so do not expect too much.

Owners get very small prize money for winning novice hurdle races or steeplechases at minor meetings (although there are more £1,000 steeplechases on the menu now) and the place money is really very poor indeed; it is surprising that we still put up with a third prize of £39, for instance, which does not even cover the cost of jockey, entry and transport. Even these little prizes are shared out in the usual way – such as 10% for the trainer and 10% for the jockey. However, the big prizes get bigger and bigger, so, as always, the lion wins the lion's share. It seems short-sighted to leave the poorer end so meagre in an effort to compete with France, where the situation is just as different as the language.

But racehorse owners are a special breed, incurably optimistic, always expecting the luck to turn, taking the rough with yet more rough, but ecstatic when things go well, believing obstinately in the merit of their horse and hoping on from one race meeting to the next.

For a very long time I found it hard to believe that I was an actual OWNER in capital letters. That character who descends on a racing stable to do a tour of inspection, loose-box door after loose-box door being opened ceremoniously, while the pedigree, achievements and glittering future of the inmates is reeled off. For a long time I felt like an interloper, knowing perfectly well the low opinion that most stable lads have of the OWNER, who often not only fails to recognize his own horse, but the lad who 'does' it! Worse still, some people even forget to put the all-important present into the right pocket as they leave. If a horse gets loose on the gallops, cast in its box, or starts to cough ominously, a visiting OWNER must contrive to vanish, or at least to move out of harm's way till order is restored. On no account should one venture: 'I suppose they all cough at this time of the year', or 'what a puffy knee'.

A tedious young woman came round the stables at Newmarket when I was staying there and managed to infer that every horse had some defect or other in an effort to display her keen interest in racing for the benefit of the boyfriend. She hadn't done quite enough homework unluckily, and as we admired a nice colt which was 'expected' next time out, she said brightly: 'This one looks as if it'll need plenty of time.' There was an icy pause, then the boyfriend's patience snapped:

'That's my best two-year-old, he's running at Ascot on Saturday. Pity you won't be there.' She wasn't.

When in doubt, it is perfectly safe to ask: 'How's he bred?' which can have no hidden dangers. It is best to avoid irritating comments like these, all of which I have overheard repeatedly:

'Personally, I don't mind four white socks.'
'I hate black horses.'
'Rather long in the back, isn't it?'
'Is that the one that fell last time out?'
'Perhaps she'll grow when the warmer weather starts.'

Saying nothing at all is dangerous too. It is of course possible to be struck dumb with the beauty-hideousness of the animal, so 'Ooh' is a safe reaction, far better than just 'oh', which could mean that you have noticed the horse's peculiar fetlocks (ankles in America, so there). If so, hurriedly stuff another Polomint into the creature's mouth while admiring its head.

A general sigh of relief follows the OWNER's car as it drives away, allowing the stable to slide back into its relentless routine. Every trainer works to a precise personal method, geared to suit the progress of each horse, but Wednesday night is traditionally bran mash night everywhere. Evening stables is specially pleasant on Wednesdays because the feed smells delicious, and a quiet munching sound, punctuated by satisfied huffles, accompanies the trainer round the horses. This is a stock-taking hour, but dedicated trainers (and they are all dedicated) go back late at night to have another look at a sick horse, or to check the bandages on a damaged leg.

Life in a racing stable starts before the birds on race days, when the runners might need to have their breakfast as early as 5 a.m. Then the first lot goes out to exercise at about 7 a.m. The day only ends when the horse-box party gets home late at night, in triumph or disappointment, from some distant venue.

The enthusiasm and hard work that everyone concerned devotes to the OWNER's interests is hard to repay and I tried to find a small extra present for the first Christmas with Auriol, thinking that a miniature bottle of Islay Mist whisky all round would be appropriate. Everywhere I went to ask – no miniatures. So in desperation I wrote to the distillery, to find a fellow racehorse owner was in charge. He most generously sent me twenty-four bottles and a large one too. He had owned a brilliant 'chaser, Even Keel, and ever since we have kept in touch over racing. (Auriol and I went to the island of Islay two years ago to find out how the whisky was getting on.)

Part of the OWNER's pleasure is seeing his horse develop from the raw materials, and raw they certainly look at first, into a racing machine. Every year Peter Thrale used to buy a cheap, 'liquorice all sorts', batch of yearlings, with extraordinary skill, and once out of fourteen, eight won races. I used to see these rough-looking babies being broken in, then at exercise, gradually improving until the butterfly popped out of its chrysalis and a racehorse emerged. We were admiring far the best of a very mixed lot one morning, when my tactless comment, 'He has knees like a jersey calf', was not welcome. Peter said 'Yes' in a most uncompromising voice. The owner was within earshot. I did not make the same mistake again.

OWNERS can be very slow to pay their bills and the

longest argument one trainer had went on for months, ending in a series of lawyers' letters, because the man who had three horses in training would neither pay his bills, nor remove the horses. Nothing would get the owner to pay, although he had plenty of money. Finally, the trainer rang him up to say that if the horses were not sent for the next afternoon, they would be left with their rugs on, but with plenty of hay and water, tied to the garden fence in full view of the passing traffic with a placard saying who owned them. The horses were fetched within the day. Non-payment of trainers' bills has ruined many small racing stables. It is very unfair indeed to run up large accounts if you cannot afford to pay, and making an arrangement with Weatherbys so that they settle all bills appears to be much the best plan.

Being an OWNER may create every sort of headache, but standing in the brilliant breezy sunshine at Folkestone races one May afternoon, without a runner for a change, I decided that on a warm, sunny day any old racehorse looks beautiful and was tempted yet again to bid for the winner of the 'Seller'. (I didn't.)

Even the disappointment over Makadir has made absolutely no difference. I love racing, there are lots of other horses, and there is always next time.

9

Very Dark

How does anyone pick the winner? Hunch, intuition, blind luck, reading the sporting papers, studying umpteen different form books? I have used a mixture of all these for many years and in 1976 was invited to join the Ladies' Twelve Club. For this, twelve horses are chosen before the flat-racing season begins, and the winner is the person whose chosen twelve wins the most races at the best odds. In 1976 my twelve managed to do just fractionally better than break even, but 1977 started very poorly for me. Most mug punters are grateful to break even at all, and reluctant to admit that their betting has not been more successful. Obviously if every horse ran true to form every time, the game would stop. There would be no possible interest and the imponderable, unpredictable factors, the horse, the jockey, the going and the hazards which are ever present at the start, even with stalls to help, would all be ironed out into a dull, uninteresting contest. Studying the form book to make your own deductions is part of the fun, but taken too literally would shake any budding owner's confidence because so few entries are encouraging.

It can be read to mean almost anything, from 'what a super horse', to 'lucky brute'. So much depends on what really happened. If you are at a race meeting, watching closely and actually noticing the way a horse has behaved, it is amusing to read what is then written about it. If the horse belongs to you, and is known to dislike hard going, you will be fascinated to read that it should do much better when the going is firm. The possible answer is that the horse would be just as bad whatever the conditions.

The form books try to report exactly what happened to every runner in every race, which can be disheartening because the reasons for failure are seldom flattering. *Timeform* is one expert aid for the punter and there is also the *Yellow Book* – which assesses the merits of every runner. With the help of these excellent publications, it should be perfectly simple to find the winner, but really the pin method is almost as successful, because horses are as fallible as the human beings who ride them.

The results, published in the racing papers, tell the bald facts and you can take your pick from the reports on a number of races that took place one day last March. I have to tell the sad truth that horses are killed quite often at jumping meetings – and that the number of serious injuries jockeys suffer is great – but just to illustrate how bad horses cost as much to keep as good ones, I have listed some actual examples of how expensive failures happened; what about:

Reluctant to race, ran out through wing fifth

Rear throughout

Fell first

Always behind, pulled up approaching two out

Never a danger

Slowly away, pulled up after fourth

Refused to race

Blundered and unseated rider fifth

Led till approaching last, faded rapidly, virtually pulled up

and so on . . .

One fact which must be faced is that only the first four in any race ever do any good. In some novice steeplechases everyone is in trouble from start to finish, till the survivors come puffing and blowing past the post, sometimes followed after a long pause by a brave jockey who has remounted and managed to get his horse to climb over the last fence before the time limit expired. On the flat the excuses/reasons are less hectic. Here is a selection to mull over in case you wonder what makes owners look so worried:

Saddle slipped, pulled up

Outpaced

Reared up at start – headway final furlong

Workmanlike – slow start

Dwelt, always behind (this has the horrible ring of utter truth)

or (even less attractive)

Sweating, always behind

No headway

Tailed off

Never placed to challenge

Swerved badly, left start, some headway halfway, never nearer

. . . bumped close home

Unseated rider leaving stalls

Never troubled leaders

Tailed off from half-way

But on the other side of the medal, there is the winner on the flat who:

Made all, comfortably;

and, over the sticks:

Looked well, led after fourth, soon clear, unchallenged.

Every trainer likes to see H. D. W. after the horse's name in a *Raceform* report, this means 'has done well' and occurs frequently at the beginning of the season as the horses reappear one year older, having grown during the winter, filled out, and generally improved. Absolutely everyone likes the little brackets that denote a win, and the little star that goes with them; unfortunately other people's horses are much better at collecting brackets than mine.

There are umpteen permutations of reasons why a horse does not win and when there are jumps to add to the difficulties it is almost impossible to believe that anyone ever could. Obstacles or no obstacles, when the form reads: 'Took no part', there is no possible shadow of doubt about that. 'Unseated rider' can mean absolutely anything. The rider could simply fall off, either because his stirrup leather broke, or the horse stopped suddenly in front of the fence to take a closer look, or the horse hit the fence hard, nearly fell on its nose and catapulted the jockey out of the saddle, or stumbled on landing, tipping the jockey neatly onto the floor. How do you know which of these things happened by just reading 'Us r.'?

It is also impossible to tell whether the horse that 'weakened in the last furlong' has weakened because it remembers being hit very hard last time out, when it was doing its best in a close finish. It could just as well have weakened because it is sickening for the cough, has sore shins, or hates the going. Incidentally, if a horse suddenly puts its head up in the last strides this usually means it can do no more.

With so many unpredictable four-legged factors to weigh up in a race, one could argue that betting is just a waste of energy (and money), but in spite of the evidence to prove this unfortunate fact, betting is a major industry, largely supported by students of form. In ideal conditions with good weather and perfect going it can be safe to follow the money and back the favourite, but human error creeps in. Time and again the jockey is blamed for either hitting the front too soon, making a move too late, getting shut in on the rails, allowing the horse to 'drop itself out', going for his whip at the wrong moment, or dropping his hands too early. In fact, only the winning jockey can be sure to earn wholehearted praise, unless he has given the horse an unnecessarily hard race, or taken a terrible risk and only just got away with it.

I have often thought a horse would have been placed if the jockey had ridden it out, but no one knows except the man in the saddle if there is anything left to ride out. Flagrant examples are sometimes spotted by the stewards, who object strongly to lack of effort in the closing stages of a race (and anywhere else in the race for that matter). It makes me furious if my each way longshot, which could have been third, fades in the last hundred yards. Unfortunately not every owner or trainer wants his horse to over-exert itself when there is no hope of winning. Some people are cleverer at arranging these little deceptions than others, and it pays to get to know whose horses are unlikely to be very busy first time out, nor yet the second time. Peter Thrale was keenly interested in horses that finished fourth in a big field, or just failed to finish fourth.

He said it was essential to note how near they actually were to the winner as it passed the post. When I was following form on the flat with real dedication, I often found a winner at a nice price by backing those 'near misses'.

Some trainers excel at producing winners first time out, but the experts usually spot these, so they tend to start at short odds, but the beginning of the season produces the oddest results, specially among untried two-year-olds. There is no limit to the possibilities of trouble with young horses. They will stand up, putting their silly feet in the most dangerous places, dash in all directions for no particular reason, and generally act as stupidly as a lot of unfenced sheep. Early in the season, two-year-olds will be heard neighing desperately as they prance round the paddock in a disorderly-looking group, but watch out for one or two sensible, sleek, grown-up individuals who look like old hands already, it is among these that the winner may be lurking. They have probably been taken to the racecourse already to get them used to travelling, and to strange places. This can be better than backing the favourite, although the money often talks pretty good sense in two-year-old races.

Once Peter Thrale ran a dreadfully plain, plump filly at Sandown, still in her shaggy winter coat, looking out of place among a select field all obviously much more forward in condition. I ventured two shillings for a place on the Tote, because she was a friendly creature, and a bright bay with a white star on her forehead like Merrylegs. She started as the absolute outsider at 50 to 1. When the tapes went up Peter's odd-looking animal dashed off along the far rails so fast that she was never headed. I got a wonderful £4 10s. for my two shillings place bet and unfortunately went up smiling to congratulate Peter while he was trying, with little or no success, to placate the owner, who much enjoyed having a nice bet. He had been told that the filly had no chance whatever; in fact she never ran well again.

One of my friends had a similar experience the first time he rode on the flat in a Bumpers' (Amateurs') race in the holidays while he was a schoolboy. He accepted a chance ride on a mare that had never run before. She was most peculiar looking with long whiskers, a shaggy coat, a slightly dipped back and a fat stomach, which provoked insulting comments from the other riders and some spectators who thought she might be in foal. The poor boy was scarlet with embarrassment as he went down to the start for his first ride in public. The other horses dashed off, leaving him trailing along behind for the first half of a two-mile race, and he was still a good way adrift when they turned for home with half a mile to go; but suddenly the mare's steady gallop began to overhaul first one horse, then another, until they reached the slope up to the finish where he was left alone in front and won easily. An enlarged photograph which hung in the hall of his house showed the mare, ears pricked, looking as surprised as everyone else as they passed the winning post. Like Peter's two-year-old, she never won again.

Long-priced, disregarded outsiders are only welcomed into the winners' enclosure by the bookies, or some owners, because even if you have not had a bet, it's pleasant to own the winner. My sister Helen backed a 50 to 1 outsider at Manchester racecourse (now closed) because one of the newspapers that her husband managed there, gave away a picture of Gordon Richards on art paper and this free gift was advertised all over the town on race day. When Helen saw that there was a horse actually called Art Paper down to run, she risked ten shillings each way on the Tote and had the win of her life.

I have a passion for forecasts (betting on one's chosen two horses to be first and second in either order), specially at

Newbury and York where they have been very lucky for me. The jackpot, on the other hand, is not so easy. The only time I found the first five winners, so did everyone else and several people got all six (now one only needs to find the last five, so I might do better). This was rather like my big moment with the Football Pools, when I got 24 points, and the excitement was unbearable – till I learnt the dividend – it was £11 10s. That was the only dividend ever to come my way after several years, except when they sent me a small sum by mistake and I returned the postal order, at which they rather pathetically rewarded me with a present of five shillings. One of my friends had a surprise win at Sandown when she was handed the wrong ticket at the Tote and decided not to go back and change it.

Colour television has added a marvellous new dimension, but watching on TV sometimes encourages me to have more than one bet, which tends to be expensive. (The expert punter bets perhaps only once in a day, to win, and certainly not every day.) Now every inch of the running can be seen and in the replay errors of judgment, hard luck stories and excuses are exposed in slow motion. This must have encouraged a better regard for the rules of racing, although the stewards seem busier than ever: perhaps their eyes are kept wider open by the film patrols. I believe there should be official paid stewards who are not racehorse owners (although a steward must stand down if he has a runner in a particular race). It has always seemed to me to be most unfair that one lot of owners should pass judgment on another's horse. Unpaid stewards of meetings could still be there to maintain standards of safety in riding, use of the whip, or the smooth running of paddock procedures; but only the judge and impartial observers should be allowed to decide the fate of a trainer, the owner's prize money, or the livelihood of a jockey.

Our traditional ways of ruling the racing world will gradually become fairer, I hope. It is easy for me to give an opinion, because no problem has arisen around any of my runners, but before the war I remember Peter was told that he must parade his best horse before a race at Ascot, although it was fearfully temperamental. He asked special permission of the stewards for it to be led down to the start after the other horses, but they refused. At least one of those stewards had a runner in the same race. This instance stuck in my mind and I wonder how unbiased anyone can be. Even the Archangel Gabriel might find it hard where horses are concerned.

The camera now helps immensely in a tight finish, but I regret the rarity of dead heats which so often gave two good horses an equal reward. Now the merest *soupçon* of a whisker decides results and early in 1977 a wrong decision on a photograph had to be reversed. Surely a dead heat could be given when there is less than one inch in it? Even when the decision is reversed later, the bets stand, which again seems unfair. But that's racing – as you may have guessed.

Newcomers to racing can be heard plaintively asking what all the numbers on their race card mean, so in case you were not brought up near or in racing circles, these few snatches of information will be useful when you first study a race card. The little numbers on the left are for the jackpot (if there is a jackpot) but, to muddle you thoroughly, the horse only has, let's say, number 9, whereas the jackpot needs to add the number of the race – for instance, 109 for the first race, 209 for the second. Please don't search in vain for 109 in the paddock, I promise it won't be there. The horse's name is followed by its colour, sex and pedigree.

Thoroughbreds come in various official colours which are puzzling to say the least, considering that whatever the lady kept saying about riding to Banbury Cross, there's no such thing as a white racehorse.

On the racecourse:

White horses are gr – grey;

Pink horses are ro – roan;

Grey horses are gr for anything from pure white to deepest charcoal (all right, I agree there's one white racehorse, and he turns bright pink with shame as soon as he gets hot – his name is White Wonder and he wins occasionally);

Brown horses are, oddly enough, br – brown;

Bright ripe-conker-coloured horses are b – bay with black trimmings – legs, mane and tail, although a few cheat by failing to have black legs;

Anything from dirty yellow to brilliant amber is ch – chestnut and these often go in for white socks and white blazes, while some have very pretty cream manes and tails;

Black horses are bl – black, but what you and I would call black is very often br, because it is the colour of the foal's muzzle that determines his official description when he is registered in the Stud Book.

Some gr horses have large white blotches which are usually inherited from the Tetrarch, who was known as the spotted wonder. I believe he was unbeaten as a two-year-old and his curious colouring crops up again and again, although there has been nothing quite as fast as the original so far.

Now that you know all about their colour, sex comes next – a male racehorse is a colt – c, till he is five, then he is officially a horse — h, unless meanwhile he has been radically altered, to put it politely, into a gelding — g. The only other alternative, and the horse prefers to draw a veil over this embarrassing predicament, is to be a rig — r, which means that there is something missing (a successful jumper with that name has been running for some years and would prefer me to go no further into the matter). A female horse is a filly — f until she is five when she becomes a mare — m.

The owners and the trainers are named, but with partnerships, two owners' names only can be listed now that up to twelve people are allowed to share one horse — the number of names that might turn up on a busy day could be impossible to fit in. The jockey's name comes on the right with the weight the horse must carry. Remember to notice if an apprentice is claiming a weight allowance, or if a famous jockey has been substituted for the rider mentioned on the card. This can be a straight tip. If the rider is described as Mr, Mrs, or Miss, he/she is an amateur, claiming up to 7 lbs. Some amateurs (jockeys too occasionally) are too heavy to do the weight and the overweight is announced on the number board; chalked up: No. 18 carries 11.12 for instance, might mean that Mr X has failed to sweat off the last few pounds in the sauna and his horse is carrying more than his share.

The only other, but most important, information on your card is the past performance of every runner. Rows of 0000 or 1111 are self-explanatory, but remember the usefulness of 04 — those two runs might be the prelude to a nice win.

The announcement that blinkers are worn by number . . . could merely mean that the horse needs to keep his mind on racing instead of staring at the crowd, the other horses, or the car park. If he is wearing a hood, i.e. a Ku Klux Klan job right over his ears, as well, this could be more sinister, and sometimes the first run in either headgear makes a nonsense of the form. I backed a 20 to 1 winner at the Curragh as a girl because it was wearing a very new hood and looked as if it had been galloping for weeks. I bravely asked the lad if the horse had worn a hood before and he glared at me and said: 'No, indeed not.' Unfortunately I was shouting my outsider home as it beat the favourite by a neck, when it dawned on me that the people I was staying with owned the favourite. They were standing in frozen silence just behind me – oh well, that's racing. Nowadays the fact that a horse is to wear blinkers must be declared overnight on the flat (not yet for National Hunt races).

Once you have sorted out the colours of the horses, the incredible variety of colours worn by the jockeys comes next. Stripes round and round are hoops, but lines up and down are stripes – isn't it simple? Pink can mean almost anything from tinned salmon to loudest fuchsia and old faded jackets once blue are often just about grey. New silks tend to look embarrassingly shiny and some owners go in for colour combinations which could well have been chosen to startle the opposition. So far no one has stitched sequins on Liberace-wise – but you never know.

If there are two horses belonging to the same owner, watch out to see which is wearing the 'second colours'. This usually means a change of cap, and it is very significant when a leading jockey is on one horse and a lesser light on the other. All the same, the oddest results do happen, so this is not an infallible tip.

The difference between the skills of star jockeys who ride on the flat and ordinary competent riders is rather like the difference between Derby horses and handicappers. The same applies at the winter game where bad riding adds to the danger – apart from ruining the career of any horse that is repeatedly jabbed hard in the mouth as it takes off, then gets a resounding thump on the spine as its rider, unbalanced on landing, bumps heavily down into the saddle. Some amateurs ride beautifully, but can be defeated in a tight finish if they come up against a professional who is bound to be a better judge of pace and knows exactly how best to time his effort. The girl riders went off far too fast when they first began to ride in races on the flat in 1973, charging along all over the place like a herd of zebras, until one of them stayed in front to win. Now they are much more skilful and most of them look confident and in control. When in doubt in Amateur races, back the best rider. In other races don't forget that the best jockeys can make the most of opportunities others would never notice, and allow an advantage of about 7 lbs in a big field for a star jockey.

The best apprentices are worth following. The 7 lbs that can be claimed before a boy has won ten flat races, the 5 lbs he can claim until he wins fifty races and the 3 lbs he claims till he has won seventy-five races are very useful – but no amount of weight advantage can help a poor sort of horse ridden by an inexperienced jockey.

Years ago, at Manchester, the three Wragg brothers and Michael Beary (all brilliant jockeys) discovered that there was a strip of concrete under the rails on the stands side, so on wet, muddy days that was where they all chose to race. I watched them edging over again and again. It took a lot of doing from a poor draw, but they won a great many races that way, with my two shillings to encourage them. When the Wraggs and Michael Beary were all riding in the same race, it was highly entertaining. Without starting stalls to ensure an even break, sheer horsemanship was the key.

Starting stalls are comparatively recent (they are still not available on every racecourse) and I am delighted by the fairness of the system. It would be difficult now for the great Sir Gordon Richards to be left at the start, as he was on the hottest favourite of all time in a two-horse race at Chepstow (I think). Without stalls a tiresome horse was able to jerk backwards as the tapes rose, allowing a wall of horses to shut him out. There were penalties for starting from the wrong place in the draw, but quite often the most respected jockeys would do this – should one assume by mistake? This occurs even now, but is much harder to achieve. Hurdle races and steeplechases are started with a flag and a starting tape, without drawing for places, and a two-mile hurdle can easily be lost at the start. Over longer distances it does not matter so much, but I am still surprised at the number of times horses refuse to race, get left at the start, or dart under the tapes out of control, and hope to goodness every time we run that it isn't my turn for this maddening, if minor, disaster.

It is fascinating to see a jockey walking along, so tiny among ordinary mortals, but transformed into a dominant force as soon as he swings into the saddle. Some, like Lester Piggott on the flat, and Andy Turnell over fences, seem to execute a supernatural balancing act which can turn into a crashing fall if the horse swerves suddenly, or stumbles.

At Ascot one day Lester, riding shorter than short, left the paddock on My Swanee, a fine performer with a strong sense of fun, who chucked him off neatly, right in front of the stands. My Swanee stood there calmly surveying the scenery, while Lester jumped up again, and when they had got half-way to the start he threw him a second time. It was all very friendly and the horse waited till Lester remounted, then stood staring into space, just thinking, in a leisurely manner, until he decided to join the other runners (he won). A horse can make his rider look ridiculous by simply doing nothing and the way it stares vacantly as if unable to understand that it is required to walk forward now, and not next week, is utterly maddening. The crosser you get, the less a horse will cooperate. I have twice seen a two-year-old get down and crawl through the front of the starting stalls, which looks impossible. But the funniest of all (if I hadn't backed him) was Scallywag, a giant colt who managed to avoid being put into the stalls by planting himself firmly, deliberately and obstinately, tight up against, and parallel with, the gate. There he stayed while a posse of dedicated handlers tried to lift first one long hard leg, then another, but the horse would not budge, and after every possible effort, short of dynamite, had been made, my selection was left behind. The horse had proved a point, because it turned out that he was so long that he could not be fitted into the starting stalls. Next time Scallywag ran, arrangements were made to fit a sort of elastic strap behind him across the gate, at which he walked in and started perfectly.

Another grey, Welsh Warrior, a favourite of mine, was an unpredictable character, who could go very fast indeed on the right day, on the right course. I decided to risk 50p on him at Epsom in a sprint and watching on TV was disappointed to see that Welsh Warrior took violent exception to the starting stalls. He would not go near them. The minutes ticked by until every handler in the place converged on the horse and heaved him bodily into the stalls. This annoyed Welsh Warrior so much that he shot off like a mad thing, led all the way and won easily. What a beauty!

The very first day of the 1977 flat season provided an example of how uncertain even the newest electrically operated gate can be if the horse plays the fool. One of these tiresome types walked in quietly enough, but decided to poke its long nose over the left side of the next stall, refusing to face the front. As the jockey struggled to pull the creature's head straight, it kept standing on its hindlegs, bouncing about until the battle ended in the jockey taking refuge on the 'step' provided in each stall to use when things get too fraught. The gate opened, and the horse crashed out riderless, to give its owner a thoroughly disappointing start to the year.

Catching a loose horse is extraordinarily difficult, because it is such a smooth, slippery shape, moves jolly fast and is not only heavy, but angular. If it happens to bump into you at speed, the result is very painful. There are few things less easy to control than an unruly, frightened thoroughbred at large in a strange place, where the railings are too high to jump easily and too solid to crash through. The horse darts about aimlessly, head and tail high, pausing now and then to take a look round, and even a bite of grass, while various officials, attendants and handlers zoom in on it, all doing their best, but getting much hotter than the horse. Every time one of them seems to be within catching distance, the waiting crowd, the other jockeys, and the starter hold their breath, hoping — but oh no, not yet. The horse swerves violently and gallops off again, just out of reach. Sometimes racing is held up for ages while this game of tag develops. It is obviously too dangerous to start a race with a loose horse dancing about on the course, because it might try to rejoin its friends at the wrong moment. Horses hate hanging about and a delay can easily affect the result of a race.

The jockey can fall off because his saddle slips, or a stirrup leather snaps, and just once in a while the bridle breaks. The last most unattractive 'hazard' is an objection, with the Stewards' Inquiry that follows. The jockey can object because his horse was bumped and bored (leant against), because his ground was taken, or he (or his horse) was hit by a rival's whip, and the stewards can object if someone has done any of these things and because of dangerous or careless riding. They can also caution and fine jockeys for over-use of the whip, can penalize them for not exerting themselves enough, or for apparently 'throwing away a race' and if the stewards consider that the rules have been seriously dented, they can stop a jockey riding for whatever period is thought to fit the 'crime'.

The trainer can lodge an objection on behalf of the owner for many of these reasons, but frivolous objections are severely discouraged by fines, so it is essential to know what one can object to effectively. I have often been tempted to object to the weather, the other horses going so fast, all the fences getting in the way and the course being too long, but I don't recommend trying it. When an objection is announced, the red flag goes up and winning bets are not paid until the result is known. As soon as all is well, the blue flag goes up, but bookies and the Tote never pay until the magic words 'Weighed in' are spoken.

Just about once I remember the winning jockey failing to weigh in, thereby losing the race, but more often the second, third or fourth fail to weigh in. The weight must be the same, within a small tolerance (2 lbs I think) before and after the race. Under no circumstances can the weight be much less. But on a rainy day, a jockey would come back dripping wet and might easily weigh a little more.

Watchers on the gallops (touts) who want to assess the merits of horses in training, can be deceived because they cannot be sure what weight each horse is carrying. I used to see 'trials' where horses were lent by other trainers to test Peter Thrale's good ones, before important races, but the weight each horse actually carried was a carefully guarded secret.

Touts try to discover every detail, and use their powers of persuasion on stable lads to extract information – most of which is pretty useless because the lads tend to indulge in wishful thinking. However, talking horses have been known to win and there is only one direction the information can come from. Owners are acknowledged to be the worst tipsters, but sometimes an aura of confidence oozes out of the 'connections' to such an extent that I am impelled to risk my 50p. I once noticed a lady wearing a new and wildly expensive fur coat with a *chapeau* (it was more than a mere hat) created to match her colours, and it seemed more than likely that she was got up to lead in the winner. I followed my hunch, to find that her horse was a hot favourite and obviously meant to oblige. It did.

If children look wildly excited (I mean worse than usual) when father's horse appears in the paddock, that can be a pointer too. The real racing-bred type of small boy, however, wears the same racing face as father, and even the same racing hat, and he gives nothing away – blending himself into the little group to the manner born, one can feel the generations stretching forward still wearing that purposeful racing expression and looking through those watchful racing eyes.

Binoculars vary as much as their wearers. Some trainers carry enormous magnifying race glasses, dripping with massed badges from racecourses all over Britain. Others glance casually through battered old binoculars, hastily snatched from a battered old case, while I let down the side by allowing my beautiful Zeiss glasses to dangle round my neck, out of harm's way, leaving the case in the car (and no messy little badges either). Every time something thrilling happens, a tall man seems to step smartly across my line of vision. At Newbury this repeated itself so often one day that when a huge body stepped right in front of me yet again and a voice said: 'Let me know if I am in your way', I answered sweetly:

'If you are, I'll cut your head off.' He disappeared.

Racegoers map out their own special 'rat-run' on a racecourse and follow it from the paddock to the Tote, to the stands, to the bar – or backwards and forwards between the bookies and the bar, with a brief pause to allow each race to interrupt their progress. The special, scuttling, hurried walk towards Tattersalls should never be halted for conversation; it is absolutely wrong to come between a punter and his betting – which is always secret. Along the rails, separating the Members from their fellow racegoers, a row of bookies spread their boards and stand waiting for the mugs to scuttle towards them. The walk back is more deliberate, as the punter waves goodbye temporarily to his/her money in the fervent hope that it will be multiplied in a few minutes. I very rarely venture into Tattersalls, it is usually farther from the paddock than the Tote and my day is largely devoted to 'counting their ears and whiskers' which means looking carefully at every horse in every race before it goes down to the start. The Tote is often in the paddock, or beside it, and just within the last year or so, betting shops have also opened near the paddock on a number of racecourses. The mug punters will be able to lose their money even faster now.

Now perhaps I could help you over the betting. My goddaughter asked why a horse called Bar was so often 10 to 1 on TV betting shows. This merely means that all the horses could be backed at 10 to 1 or better, except those listed at shorter odds.

I have learnt that it very often pays to put a Tote place bet on the favourite. When money was a real problem, I relied on these frankly timid investments to earn me my entrance money. The favourite is not very often beaten out of the first three and a modest return is better than nothing. But there are few things nicer than plain winning bets at a long price, and the fact that these are so few and far between makes finding the winner all the more rewarding.

10

You Can Take a Horse to the Water . . .

Having managed to prevent my lifelong career in the wonderful world of women's magazines from interfering with my racing, I must admit that it was only working with magazines that allowed me to be prosperous enough to be a racehorse owner. It took well over forty years from the day when I dreamt the winner of the Grand National in 1930, to that magic morning in 1970 when I first met Islay Mist.

It was at Kempton in 1971 that I proudly wore my first owner's badge, feeling at long last part of the racing pattern and not only a dedicated onlooker. In 1972 my whole racing life changed radically, because holidays began to be shaped round Islay Mist's activities in the south of England in the spring and autumn, while we kept one week in the summer to go exploring racecourses, picking a base with two possible race meetings near by, which took us all over the country.

Ashdown Forest, in her turn, added Brighton, Newbury, Haydock and Worcester to our collection, while Makadir took us as far and wide as Nottingham, Ascot, Sandown, Towcester, Huntingdon and Warwick. It is impossible to count up the thousands of miles we covered on those many wild-goose chases, to stand about in a state of quivering anticipation (remember that when Makadir ran it was nearly always raining).

It is difficult to say which of the horses in my life I really loved the best. Certainly it's a dead heat between Merrylegs and Foalie (who was like a child to me), then comes Islay Mist whose book you have been reading, and after them Jane, then Makadir. Ashdown Forest, like Disobedience, although charming to look at, was never such a personal friend, she is far too temperamental to be lovable, but darling Mak is different. He comes when he is called (with or without Polomints), likes to be patted, and is quiet in the stable. If only we owned a field instead of a roof garden on Campden Hill he could spend the rest of his life idling there. Which brings me to one absolutely crucial problem that has simply got to be faced. What do you do with a thoroughly reluctant racehorse? You can't just leave him in a handy field, specially if you live in London – there aren't enough fields to go round, and he is used to care and attention at all times. You can't very well wrap him up and send him to someone for Christmas, or just wish he would go away. Your horse is there, all sixteen hands of him, needing to be fed and watered, so perhaps you decide to sell him, and this is when you discover that there is all the difference in the world between buying a horse and selling a horse. Let us go to see Racehorse A with a view to buying him. He is in training at a reputable establishment, impeccably bred, available, and has run quite well on the flat. Enquiries reveal that he has never been sick or sorry – he is as sound as a bell, quiet as a lamb in the stable and a good ride for a boy/girl/person. Loves racing – tries every inch of the way and has a great turn of foot. Doesn't mind what the going is like and although not in the first rank (he has won nothing) is full of quality and has infinite potential.

Allowing yourself to wonder momentarily why this paragon is about to be sold, you put all baser thoughts aside and rush to see the beast in an agony of worry. Perhaps someone else will want to buy him – perhaps the owner doesn't really mean to sell. Then the fun begins.

Standing in the loose-box awaiting your inspection is a large four-legged creature with a long tail, two pointed little ears and a shiny neck. That is about all you can see at first, because a thick canvas rug covers everything else and his head is away in the darkest corner, firmly attached to a stable person who is determined to keep everything neat, quiet and controlled throughout. With a gesture born of long practice, the trainer steps forward and, as if unveiling a priceless treasure, flips the rug away to reveal the glistening beauty of the horse's loins. As you gasp in admiration, the stable person quickly undoes a few buckles and deftly bares the whole magnificent expanse. It is indeed a racehorse you are admiring, but it wants to come outside for a nice breath of air, so you back away hurriedly while everyone carries on with the supposition that it is a quiet, well-behaved thoroughbred, without a trace of *arrière pensée*, malice or even sense of humour (horses need all the sense of humour available to them when you think of the bundles of nonsense they must listen to whenever people talk about them within earshot).

As the horse dashes, slithers, stumbles, charges, or minces elegantly into the yard, a blow by blow biography is trotted out at lightning speed by the trainer. 'He's by Jingo out of Bagwash by Serge Panz who goes back to Jericho, who won the big race at Ullapool in record time, and an own brother to Bang On who actually never ran, but would have won the Derby only he broke his neck.'

The horse, fidgeting under your critical gaze and consuming Polomints by the handful, seems perfectly adequate. Rather small perhaps, with a meek but obstinate expression and flat feet. A small lump on one leg is explained away quickly – so is a long scar on the near hindquarter. A hint of temper whenever a Polomint is not at once forthcoming seems unimportant – and a dry cough hardly worth mentioning. It is a wonderful little horse – so compact, neat, well made, unlikely to sprawl, easy to train, easy to place, ready to win a nice little race in a few weeks. Just the job for a new owner who wants success to come soon. Why hesitate? This is the horse for you.

Now try to sell the same animal and you soon learn the facts of life. It appears that your horse is a bit small, far from powerful, not really fashionably bred, he may prove difficult to place and appears unlikely to grow on. His legs are far from perfect, his temperament questionable and at any moment he may have to be turned into cat's meat.

This is the gypsy's warning and, as my uncle often said: 'Don't start what you can't stop.' If you cannot picture clearly the eventual fate of an unsuccessful racehorse, don't buy one. Lease a horse instead, for its racing career. This means that you are responsible for training fees, insurance and all costs of keeping the horse while it is racing, but it returns whence it came afterwards. Some leases have the cheering proviso that after the first £5,000 has been won, the prize money is shared. I might even settle for that, although it is not the same thing, not so personal as being the owner of the horse. But as always, yet another venture is possible. I might decide to send Makadir hunter 'chasing instead. Hunter 'chasers must have been out with a pack of hounds regularly, and cannot appear on a racecourse after 1st November. The season for them only lasts from February to June, so there are just four months in which to stand about in the rain, agonizing. I intend to discuss this with Makadir quite soon, hoping he may decide to take up this new career instead of being sold, because I cannot support him in luxury indefinitely.

Looking back over six years of tremendous involvement, great enjoyment and hard worry, with rather more downs than ups, there are no regrets; instead a sense of having fulfilled an ambition very much more completely than I ever dared to hope. There is nothing to equal the thrill of leading in your first winner, and as far as I am concerned, no matter how many beautiful thoroughbreds may join my family (in strictly limited doses of course) no horse could ever have the same mystique for me as Islay Mist. I can still picture him streaking past the winning post at Plumpton to give me the great satisfaction of leading him in.

Racing takes on a new dimension when you become even an infinitesimal fragment of the jigsaw – and as a spectator the triumphs and disasters will be heightened for evermore because you have experienced them at first hand. A worrying situation develops as soon as friends realize that your horse is running. They all immediately expect it to win, every time too – whatever you may say about the creature's chances, the keenness of absolutely everyone to have a flutter is not to be denied. No wonder the bookies seem to breed Rolls-Royces. Please don't back a horse simply because you happen to know the owner, and double please don't ever venture one penny more than you can afford to lose. Decide on a stake and when that has melted away – stop. That is how I managed to survive with my bank balance only slightly bruised all through the years when Peter kept describing me as a desperate character when I marched away towards the Tote to risk my two shillings. After all this time I still love looking at horses, talking about horses with my partner, picking out the winner (or trying to!) in the paddock, and thinking about the next race. There are never any regrets, except that Islay Mist died so young.

As soon as the new season starts I shall be longing to get back into this maddening, exhilarating, fascinating and unrewarding game, so watch out for sky blue, white crossbelts, black and blue hooped cap. There's always another day – that's racing.